# The BIG BOOK of Civil War Quilts

## 58 Patterns for Reproduction-Fabric Lovers

Martingale®
Create with Confidence

The Big Book of Civil War Quilts:
58 Patterns for Reproduction-Fabric Lovers
© 2017 by Martingale & Company®

Martingale®
19021 120th Ave. NE, Ste. 102
Bothell, WA 98011-9511 USA
ShopMartingale.com

Printed in China
22 21 20 19 18 17          8 7 6 5 4 3 2 1

Library of Congress Cataloging-in-Publication Data
is available upon request.

ISBN: 978-1-60468-855-9

## MISSION STATEMENT

We empower makers who use fabric and yarn to make life more enjoyable.

## CREDITS

PUBLISHER AND
CHIEF VISIONARY OFFICER
Jennifer Erbe Keltner

CONTENT DIRECTOR
Karen Costello Soltys

MANAGING EDITOR
Tina Cook

ACQUISITIONS EDITOR
Karen M. Burns

COPY EDITOR
Melissa Bryan

DESIGN MANAGER
Adrienne Smitke

COVER AND
INTERIOR DESIGNER
Regina Girard

PHOTOGRAPHER
Brent Kane

# Contents

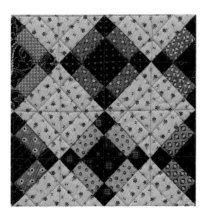

# Introduction

When it comes to working with reproduction fabrics, we know one thing for certain—many quilters just can't get enough of them. And we understand that, because we can't either!

Many of Martingale's best-selling authors are just like you. They love the rich colors and the prints that range from endearing to downright funky. They love combining those fabrics in ways generations of women did before us. There's a reason that their books, featuring reproduction fabrics, are some of our most popular.

Whether you're new to the "reproduction club" or have been quilting with fabrics from the Civil War era for years, we're sure you'll find much to love about this book. It's packed with options that can help you use up your treasured stash of reproduction fabrics—and have you clamoring to buy more!

Are you in need of a bed-size quilt to welcome guests and help them have sweet dreams during their visit? Or a lap-size quilt to snuggle under in your family room? Or perhaps making a small quilt or two to round out your favorite display of collectibles is on the horizon. Whatever you're itching to make, we're pretty sure we've got you covered, with 58 patterns from the likes of Kim Diehl, Country Threads, Carol Hopkins, Jo Morton, and many more amazing designers.

So dive in, peruse the options, and then get ready to have some sewing fun. The only decision you'll need to face is which pattern to make first!

# Black and Beyond

**FINISHED QUILT:** 59" × 75" • **FINISHED BLOCK:** 11" × 11"

*Designed and made by Evelyn Sloppy*

*A collection of far-from-basic blacks and grays provide the foundation for this bold design. Construction consists primarily of strip-set segments, set off by stars of a brilliant red print that really enhances the vintage look of this quilt.*

## Materials

*Yardage is based on 42"-wide fabric. Fat quarters are 18" × 21"; fat eighths are 9" × 21".*

4 yards *total* OR 16 fat quarters of assorted light to medium gray prints for blocks and sashing

1½ yards *total* OR 12 fat eighths of assorted black prints for blocks and sashing

1¾ yards of red print for sashing

⅝ yard of fabric for binding

3¾ yards of fabric for backing

63" × 79" piece of batting

## Cutting

*All measurements include ¼"-wide seam allowances.*

**From the gray prints, cut a *total* of:**

40 strips, 1½" × 21"

2 strips, 2½" × 21"

26 strips, 3½" × 21"; crosscut *16 strips* into:
- 14 rectangles, 3½" × 11½"
- 18 rectangles, 3½" × 5½"
- 4 squares, 3½" × 3½"

22 strips, 4½" × 21"

**From the black prints, cut a *total* of:**

59 strips, 1½" × 21"

**From the red print, cut:**

3 strips, 5½" × 42"; crosscut into 20 squares, 5½" × 5½"

13 strips, 3" × 42"; crosscut into 160 squares, 3" × 3"

**From the binding fabric, cut:**

7 strips, 2½" × 42"

## Making the Blocks and Sashing Units

Press the seam allowances as indicated by the arrows, or as otherwise instructed.

1 Sew the two gray 2½"-wide strips and one black 1½"-wide strip together along their long edges to make a strip set. Crosscut the strip set into 12 segments, 1½" wide.

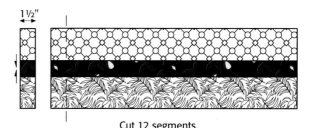

1½"

Cut 12 segments.

2 Sew five 1½"-wide strips of black and gray prints together as shown. Make five strip sets with black strips on the outside and three strip sets with gray strips on the outside. Crosscut the black strip sets into 24 segments, 3½" wide, and crosscut the gray strip sets into 24 segments, 2½" wide.

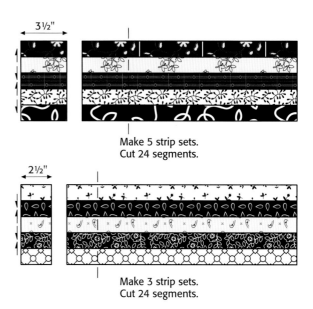

3½"

Make 5 strip sets.
Cut 24 segments.

2½"

Make 3 strip sets.
Cut 24 segments.

**3** Sew together three black 1½"-wide strips, two gray 1½"-wide strips, and two gray 3½"-wide strips as shown. Make five strip sets. Crosscut the strip sets into 24 segments, 3½" wide.

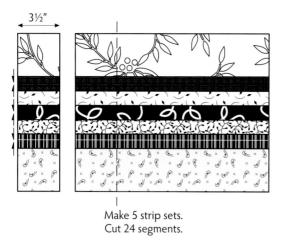

Make 5 strip sets.
Cut 24 segments.

**4** Sew one segment from step 1 and two of the 2½"-wide segments from step 2 together as shown. Then add two of the 3½"-wide segments from step 2, and finally two of the segments from step 3. The block should measure 11½" square, including seam allowances. Repeat to make 12 blocks.

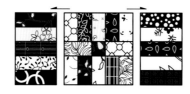

Make 12.

**5** Sew two gray 4½"-wide strips, two black 1½"-wide strips, and one gray 1½"-wide strip together as shown. Make 11 strip sets. Crosscut the strip sets into 31 segments, 5½" wide.

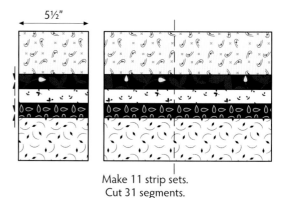

Make 11 strip sets.
Cut 31 segments.

**6** Draw a diagonal line from corner to corner on the wrong side of the red 3" squares. Place marked squares on diagonally opposite corners of a segment from step 5, right sides together and corners aligned. Sew on each drawn line. Trim the excess fabric, leaving ¼" seam allowances, and press. Repeat on the two remaining corners of the segment. Make 31. Set aside the remaining marked red squares for the border blocks.

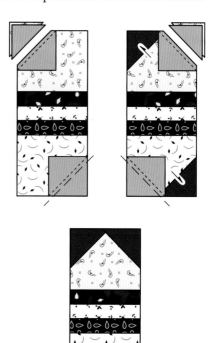

Make 31.

## Assembling the Quilt Top

1 Lay out the blocks, sashing units, and red 5½" squares in rows as shown.

2 Sew the pieces together into rows, and then join the rows.

3 Using the remaining marked red squares and referring to step 6 of "Making the Blocks and Sashing Units" on page 7, sew red squares to two corners of a gray 3½" × 5½" rectangle as shown. Repeat to make 18 border blocks.

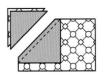 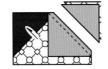

Make 18.

4 Sew together five border blocks and four gray 3½" × 11½" rectangles in alternating positions. Make two for the side borders. Sew together four border blocks and three gray 3½" × 11½" rectangles, and add a gray 3½" square to each end. Make two for the top and bottom borders. Sew the side borders to the quilt top first, and then add the top and bottom borders.

## Finishing the Quilt

Refer to "Finishing Techniques" on page 236 for details on the following steps.

1 Layer and baste your quilt, and quilt as desired.

2 Using the 2½"-wide binding strips, prepare and attach the binding.

# Another Mosaic

**FINISHED QUILT:** 44½" × 60½" • **FINISHED BLOCK:** 8" × 8"

*Designed and made by Gayle Bong*

*While this is an old block done in 1800s reproduction prints, the construction is thoroughly modern. To update the assembly, Gayle Bong incorporated folded corners and sandwich-pieced triangles she calls Twin Peaks. For a different look, pair 1930s prints with solid-colored pinwheels.*

## Materials

*Yardage is based on 42"-wide fabric.*

2⅝ yards of assorted cream prints for background
2¼ yards *total* of assorted medium and dark prints for pinwheels and trapezoids
½ yard of fabric for binding
3 yards of fabric for backing
50" × 66" piece of batting

## Cutting

*All measurements include ¼"-wide seam allowances.*

**From the assorted cream prints, cut:**

6 strips, 2⅞" × 42"; cut each strip in half to yield 12 strips, 2⅞" × 21"
9 strips, 2½" × 42"; crosscut into 140 squares, 2½" × 2½"
5 strips, 5¼" × 42"; crosscut into 35 squares, 5¼" × 5¼". Cut the squares into quarters diagonally to yield 140 triangles.
7 strips, 2½" × 42"; crosscut into:
- 20 rectangles, 2½" × 9¼"
- 8 rectangles, 2½" × 7¼"

**From the medium and dark prints, cut:**

12 strips, 2⅞" × 19"
70 squares, 4⅞" × 4⅞"; cut the squares in half diagonally to yield 140 triangles
24 squares, 2⅞" × 2⅞"; cut the squares in half diagonally to yield 48 triangles

**From the binding fabric, cut:**

6 strips, 2¼" × 42"

## Making the Blocks

Press the seam allowances as indicated by the arrows, or as otherwise instructed.

1 Place a medium or dark 2⅞" × 19" strip on top of a cream 2⅞" × 21" strip with right sides together. Sew the strips together along both long edges as shown. Press to set the seams. Repeat to make 12 strip sets. Crosscut the strip sets into 70 squares, 2⅞" each. Cut each square in half diagonally to yield 140 Twin Peaks units. Cut all of the strip sets with the dark fabric on top and be sure to cut all diagonals in the same direction as shown.

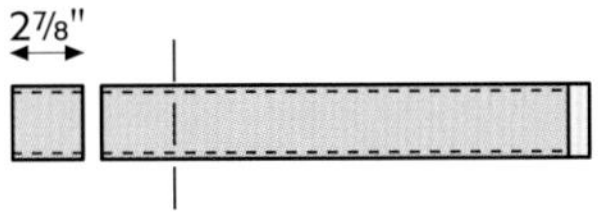


Make 12 strip sets.
Cut 70 segments.

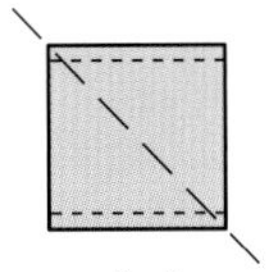

Cut all pieces at this angle.

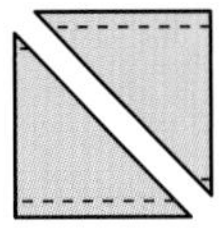

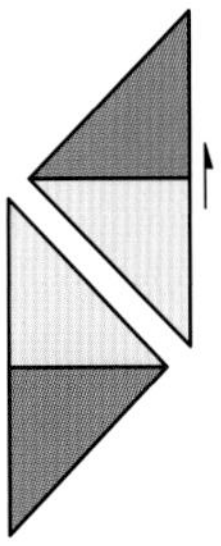

Make 140 Twin Peaks units.

### CAREFUL CUTTING

There are a couple of ways to cut the Twin Peaks pieces incorrectly, but only one way to cut them correctly. Make sure your piece placement matches the diagram *before* you cut through the corners of the square.

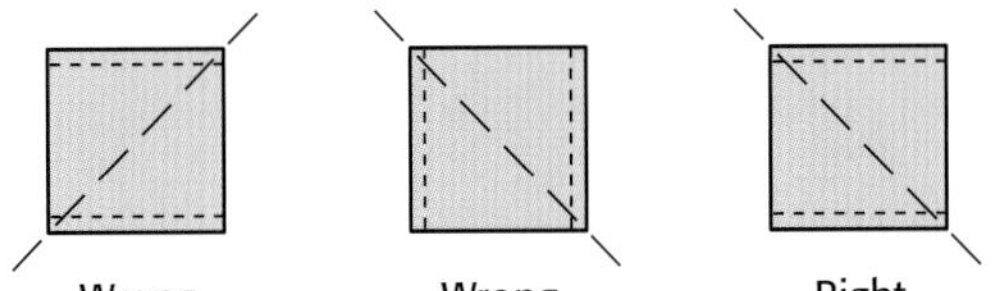

Wrong    Wrong    Right

2 Sew a cream 5¼" triangle to a Twin Peaks unit as shown. Repeat to make 140 triangle units.

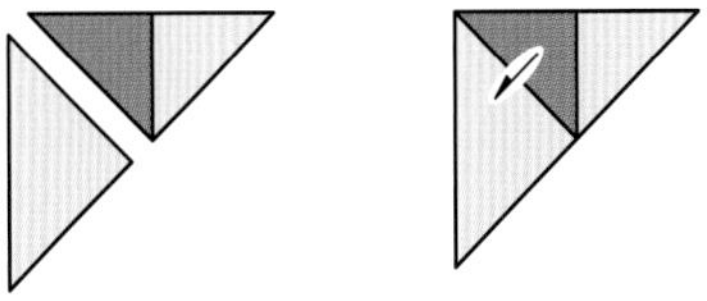

Make 140.

3 Draw a diagonal line from corner to corner on the cream 2½" squares. Place a marked square on the right-angle corner of a medium or dark 4⅞" triangle, right sides together and corners aligned. Sew on the drawn line. Trim the excess fabric, leaving ¼" seam allowances, and press. Repeat to make 140 units.

Make 140.

4 Sew the units from steps 2 and 3 together along the long edges.

5 Join four units with identical pinwheel triangles into pairs, and sew the pairs into a block. Before pressing, undo two stitches in the seam allowance at the center of the block. This will let the seam allowances fall open in a pinwheel fashion, helping to distribute the bulk at the center of the block. Press as shown. Repeat to make 35 blocks.

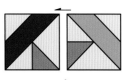
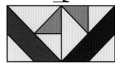
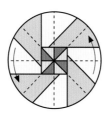

Press the seam allowance open.

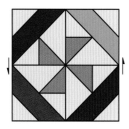

Make 35.

## Assembling the Quilt Top

1 Arrange the blocks in seven rows of five blocks each as shown in the quilt assembly diagram on page 13. When you are happy with the color arrangement, sew the blocks into rows and press the seam allowances in opposite directions from row to row. Sew the rows together and press the seam allowances in one direction.

2 Aligning the 45° line of a ruler with the bottom of each rectangle as shown, trim a 45° triangle from each end of the cream 2½" × 9¼" and 2½" × 7¼" rectangles. Make a total of 28 trapezoids.

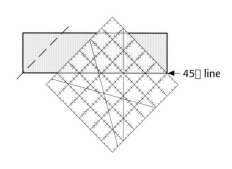

45° line

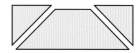

3 Sew a medium or dark 2⅞" triangle to each end of a 9¼" trapezoid. Press the seam allowances in one direction. Repeat to make 20 units.

Make 20.

4 Sew a medium or dark 2⅞" triangle to one end of a 7¼" trapezoid. Repeat to make four units with the triangle on the right side and four with the triangle on the left.

Make 4.          Make 4.

5 Join the trapezoid units to make four border strips as shown. Begin and end each border with one of the end units made in step 4.

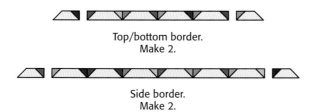

Top/bottom border.
Make 2.

Side border.
Make 2.

6 Pin the border strips to the quilt, matching centers, quarter points, and ends. Sew the borders to the quilt, easing to fit, and begin and end your stitching ¼" from each corner. This will allow for the mitered seam at the corner. Backstitch to secure the seams. Sew the diagonal seam in the corner, keeping the seam allowance free. (Visit ShopMartingale.com/HowtoQuilt if you would like illustrated instructions about mitered borders.) Press the seam allowances toward the border strips.

7 Sew a line of stay stitching ³⁄₁₆" from the edges of the quilt top to prevent the seams in the pieced border from coming loose.

## Finishing the Quilt

Refer to "Finishing Techniques" on page 236 for details on the following steps.

1 Layer and baste your quilt, and quilt as desired.

2 Using the 2¼"-wide binding strips, prepare and attach the binding.

Quilt assembly

*Another Mosaic*

# Beloved

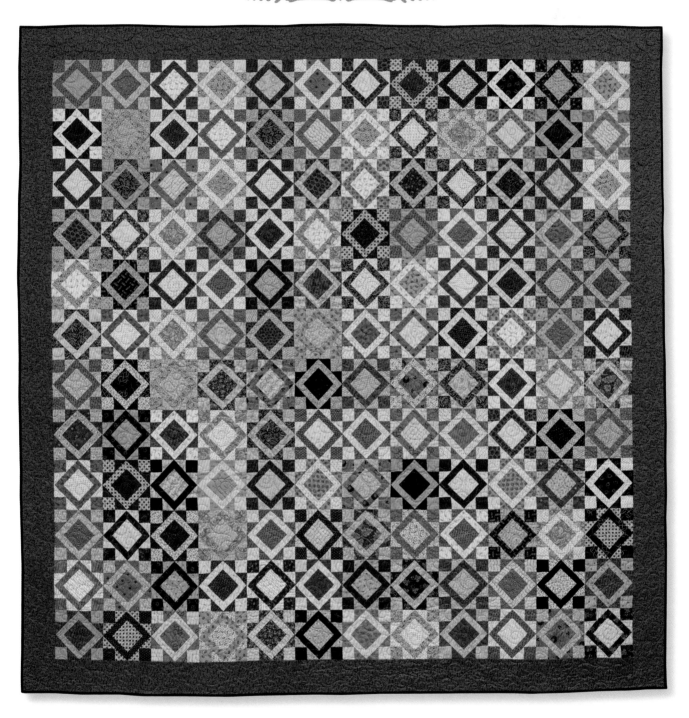

**FINISHED QUILT:** 80½" × 80½" • **FINISHED BLOCK:** 6" × 6"

*Designed and made by Rebecca Silbaugh*

*Inspired by the motto "Do one thing and do it well," designer Rebecca Silbaugh featured one block that repeats itself in a variety of different fabrics. This simple approach provides the opportunity to play with color and texture for striking results.*

## Materials

*Yardage is based on 42"-wide fabric. Fat eighths are 9" × 21"; fat quarters are 18" × 21".*

36 fat eighths OR 18 fat quarters of assorted light prints for blocks

36 fat eighths OR 18 fat quarters of assorted dark prints for blocks

1⅓ yards of green print for border

⅔ yard of black print for binding

7½ yards of fabric for backing

88" × 88" piece of batting

## Cutting

*All measurements include ¼"-wide seam allowances. Keep the pieces separated by fabric.*

**From each of the 36 light and 36 dark fat eighths, cut:***

1 strip, 4¾" × 20"; cut into:
- 4 rectangles, 1¼" × 4¾" (144 light and 144 dark)
- 8 squares, 2" × 2" (288 light and 288 dark)
- 4 rectangles, 2" × 3" (144 light and 144 dark)

1 strip, 3¼" × 20"; cut into:
- 4 rectangles, 1¼" × 3¼" (144 light and 144 dark)
- 2 squares, 3¼" × 3¼" (72 light and 72 dark)
- 4 rectangles, 2" × 3" (144 light and 144 dark)

**From the green print, cut:**

9 strips, 4½" × 42"

**From the black print, cut:**

9 strips, 2¼" × 42"

*\*If you're using fat quarters, cut twice as many pieces from each fabric.*

## Assembling the Block Sets

1. From the pieces cut from *each* light and dark fat eighth, create two A sets and two B sets as follows:

   **Each A set contains:**
   2 rectangles, 1¼" × 4¾"
   2 rectangles, 1¼" × 3¼"
   4 squares, 2" × 2"

   **Each B set contains:**
   1 square, 3¼" × 3¼"
   4 rectangles, 2" × 3"

2. Pair each light A set with a dark B set and each dark A set with a light B set. Make a total of 144 combined sets.

## Making the Blocks

Press the seam allowances as indicated by the arrows, or as otherwise instructed.

1. Working with one combined set of A and B pieces, sew the 1¼" × 3¼" rectangles to opposite sides of the 3¼" square. Sew the 1¼" × 4¾" rectangles to the remaining sides of the square. The center unit should measure 4¾" square, including seam allowances.

2 Sew each 2" square to a 2" × 3" rectangle. Make four units.

Make 4.

3 Sew two units from step 2 together as shown. Make two.

Make 2.

4 Carefully clip the seam allowances in the center of each unit from step 3, clipping up to, but *not through,* the stitching. Each pieced unit should measure 3½" × 4½", including seam allowances.

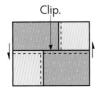

Clip.

5 Lay a pieced unit from step 4 right side down on your cutting mat and align the 45° mark on your ruler along the long edge of the unit. Line up the edge of the ruler with a corner of the unit and the intersection of the stitching on the corner square. Lightly mark the diagonal line. Rotate the unit 180° and mark the opposite corner. The marked lines should be slightly more than ½" apart. Repeat to mark the remaining unit from step 4.

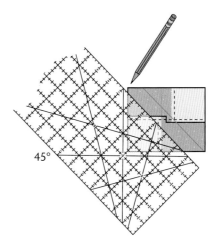

45°

6 Cut between the drawn lines of each unit, ¼" from the seam intersections, to create four corner units.

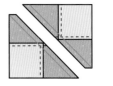 

Make 4.

### FABRIC VALUES

A common error when choosing fabrics for scrappy quilts is picking out fabrics that are too similar. Within each color you should have a mix of values. Feel free to combine prints and textures to do this. The lightest and darkest prints of each color value should almost be able to blend with the other color values in the quilt.

To get the right mix, it all comes down to how the fabrics are paired up. For example, a dark green fabric is a dark value when paired with a light tan. However, if paired with black, it might be a medium value. Just make sure there's a decent contrast between the fabrics being sewn together, and the end result will look magical.

7 Find and pin-mark the midpoint of opposite sides of the center unit from step 1. Match the center of the cut edge of a corner unit from step 6 to the pinned midpoint of the square. Pin the square and corner units and sew them together. Repeat to add a second unit as shown.

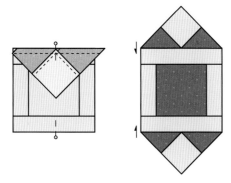

8 Sew the two remaining corner units to the remaining sides of the unit from step 7. Carefully clip the seam allowances on both sides of each corner unit's square. To reduce bulk in the seam allowances, press the clipped center toward the center square and the outer seam allowances toward the corner unit. The block should measure 6½" square, including seam allowances.

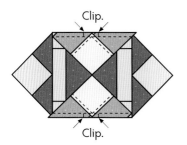

Clip.

Clip.

9 Repeat steps 1–8 to make 144 blocks. Once you get into a rhythm, the piecing will go fast. If it helps to ease the mental burden of so many blocks, set a manageable goal for yourself and piece a few every day.

## CRAYON BOX THEORY

Scrappy quilts offer the perfect opportunity to play with color. When selecting colors, take designer Rebecca Silbaugh's advice and think of a crayon box. You might not love every color of crayon, but when they're all in the box together, the effect is undeniably nice.

If you blend a few fabrics that you merely *like* with fabrics you absolutely *love*, the end result will be spectacular. More times than not, once the quilt is complete, the fabrics you didn't exactly love in the beginning will be the icing on the cake. They tend to create those little pops of something we didn't know was missing in the first place.

## Assembling the Quilt Top

1 Referring to the quilt assembly diagram on page 18, lay out the blocks in 12 rows of 12 blocks each, alternating the light and dark block centers in each row and from row to row.

2 Sew the blocks together into rows; press. Sew the rows together and press the seam allowances away from the center row.

3 Sew the green 4½"-wide strips together end to end to make one long strip. Measure the length of the quilt top through the center. Cut two green strips to this measurement and sew them to the sides of the quilt top. Measure the width of the quilt top through the center, including the borders just added. Cut two green strips to this measurement and sew them to the top and bottom of the quilt top.

## Finishing the Quilt

Refer to "Finishing Techniques" on page 236 for details on the following steps.

1 Layer and baste your quilt, and quilt as desired.

2 Using the black 2¼"-wide strips, prepare and attach the binding.

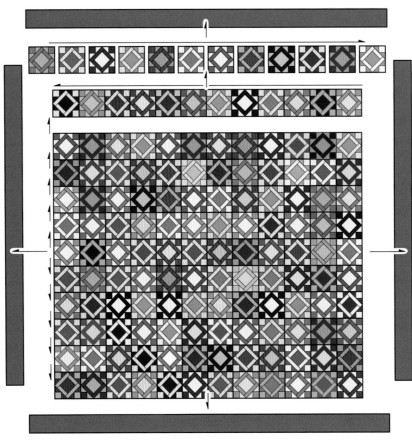

Quilt assembly

# Troops in Formation

**FINISHED QUILT:** 26½" × 32½" • **FINISHED BLOCK:** 4" × 4"

*Designed and made by Mary Etherington and Connie Tesene*

*The uniform peaks on these Delectable Mountain blocks give the impression of soldiers marching in formation, a Civil War sight that attracted somber respect whether in the rolling hills of Pennsylvania and Virginia or the rugged terrain of North Carolina.*

## Materials

*Yardage is based on 42"-wide fabric.*

8 light prints, ⅛ yard each, for blocks and pieced outer border

½ yard *total* of assorted medium or dark prints in red, blue, black, gold, and rust for blocks and pieced outer border

4 red prints, ⅛ yard each, for blocks

4 blue prints, ⅛ yard each, for blocks

⅔ yard of brown fabric for setting triangles, inner border, corner squares, and binding

1 yard of fabric for backing

30" × 36" piece of batting

## Cutting

*All measurements include ¼"-wide seam allowances.*

**From the light prints, cut:**

16 squares, 3⅞" × 3⅞"; cut the squares in half diagonally to yield 32 triangles

150 squares, 1⅞" × 1⅞"; cut the squares in half diagonally to yield 300 triangles

32 squares, 1½" × 1½"

**From the assorted medium and dark prints, cut:**

150 squares, 1⅞" × 1⅞"; cut the squares in half diagonally to yield 300 triangles

**From the red prints, cut:**

8 squares, 3⅞" × 3⅞"; cut the squares in half diagonally to yield 16 triangles

**From the blue prints, cut:**

8 squares, 3⅞" × 3⅞"; cut the squares in half diagonally to yield 16 triangles

**From the brown fabric, cut:**

1 strip, 7" × 42"; cut into:
- 4 squares, 7" × 7"; cut the squares into quarters diagonally to yield 16 triangles (2 are extra)
- 2 squares, 5½" × 5½"; cut the squares in half diagonally to yield 4 triangles

4 squares, 1½" × 1½"

4 strips, 1" × 42"

3 strips, 2¼" × 42"

## Making the Blocks

Press the seam allowances as indicated by the arrows, or as otherwise instructed.

1 Sew a light 1⅞" triangle to a dark 1⅞" triangle. Make six.

Make 6.

2 Sew a light 3⅞" triangle to a red or blue 3⅞" triangle.

Make 1.

3 Join a light 1½" square, the six units from step 1, and the unit from step 2. The block should measure 4½" square, including seam allowances. Make 32 blocks.

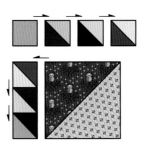 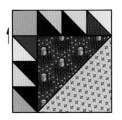

Make 32.

## Assembling the Quilt Top

1 Arrange the blocks, side triangles, and corner triangles in diagonal rows. Sew the blocks and side triangles in diagonal rows. Join the rows and add the corner triangles last. Trim the corner triangles ¼" beyond the corner of the blocks.

Quilt assembly

2 Measure the length of the quilt top through the center. Cut two brown 1"-wide strips to this measurement, and sew them to the sides of the quilt top. Measure the width of the quilt top through the center, including the borders just added. Cut two brown 1"-wide strips to this measurement and sew them to the top and bottom of the quilt. For the pieced border to fit correctly, the quilt top should be 24½" × 30½", including seam allowances. Trim the quilt top as needed to get this measurement.

3 Sew the remaining light and dark 1⅞" triangles together. Press the seam allowances toward the dark triangles. Make 108 units. Sew 24 half-square-triangle units together, orienting the dark triangles in the same direction. Make two for the top and bottom borders. Sew 30

half-square-triangle units together in the same manner, and sew a brown 1½" square to each end. Make two for the side borders.

Make 2.

Make 2.

4 Sew the top and bottom borders to the quilt top, orienting the dark triangles toward the quilt center. Sew the side borders to the quilt top in the same manner.

Quilt plan

## Finishing the Quilt

Refer to "Finishing Techniques" on page 236 for details on the following steps.

1 Layer and baste your quilt, and quilt as desired.

2 Using the brown 2¼"-wide strips, prepare and attach the binding.

# Twilight Hopscotch

**FINISHED QUILT:** 62½" × 62½" • **FINISHED BLOCK:** 12" × 12"

*Designed by Kim Diehl; pieced by Deb Behrend; quilted by Delene Kohler*

*Twinkling stars appear to be just a hop, a skip, and a jump away as they dance through the milky twilight in this traditionally designed quilt. Quiet yet eloquent, these simply pieced stars will shine in any setting.*

## Materials

*Yardage is based on 42"-wide fabric.*

1½ yards of medium green print A for blocks (stars) and binding

3½ yards of cream print for block backgrounds and sashing

1⅛ yards of medium green print B for blocks (small diagonal corner squares) and sashing squares

4 yards of fabric for backing

69" × 69" piece of batting

## Cutting

*All measurements include ¼"-wide seam allowances.*

**From medium green print A, cut:**

15 strips, 2½" × 42"; crosscut *8 strips* into 128 squares, 2½" × 2½"

2 strips, 4½" × 42"; crosscut into 16 squares, 4½" × 4½"

**From the cream print, cut:**

8 strips, 4½" × 42"; crosscut into 64 squares, 4½" × 4½"

10 strips, 1½" × 42"

26 strips, 2½" × 42"; crosscut into:
- 157 squares, 2½" × 2½"
- 40 rectangles, 2½" × 8½"
- 16 rectangles, 2½" × 12½"

**From medium green print B, cut:**

10 strips, 1½" × 42"

7 strips, 2½" × 42"; crosscut into 100 squares, 2½" × 2½"

## Making the Blocks and Sashing Units

Press the seam allowances as indicated by the arrows, or as otherwise instructed.

1 Draw a diagonal line from corner to corner on the wrong side of the 128 green A 2½" squares designated for stars. Place a marked square on one corner of a cream 4½" square, right sides together and corners aligned. Sew on the drawn line. Trim the excess fabric, leaving ¼" seam allowances, and press. In the same manner, add a second green A square in a mirror-image position. Repeat for a total of 64 star-point units.

Make 64.

2 Sew each cream 1½" × 42" strip to a green B 1½" × 42" strip along one long edge to make a strip set. Repeat for a total of 10 strip sets. Crosscut the strip sets into 256 segments, 1½" wide.

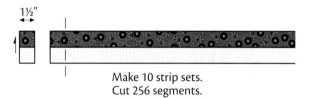

1½"

Make 10 strip sets.
Cut 256 segments.

3 Join two strip-set segments as shown to make a four-patch unit. Repeat for a total of 128 four-patch units measuring 2½" square, including seam allowances.

Make 128.

4 Lay out two four-patch units and two cream 2½" squares as shown. Join the pieces in each row, and then join the rows. Repeat for a total of 64 corner units.

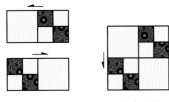

Make 64.

5 Lay out four star-point units from step 1, four corner units from step 4, and one green A 4½" square as shown, paying close attention to the orientation of the corner units. Join the pieces into rows, and then join the rows. Repeat for a total of 16 Star blocks measuring 12½" square, including seam allowances.

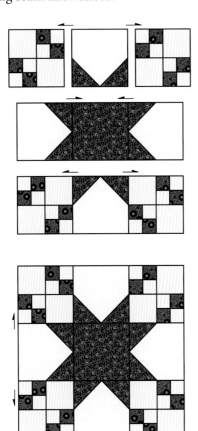

Make 16.

6 Join a green B 2½" square to each end of a cream 2½" × 8½" rectangle. Repeat for a total of 40 pieced sashing units.

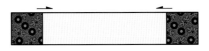

Make 40.

## Assembling the Quilt Top

1 Sew together four Star blocks and five sashing units in alternating positions. Repeat for a total of four block rows.

Make 4.

2 Sew together four sashing units and five cream 2½" squares in alternating positions. Repeat for a total of five sashing rows.

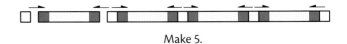

Make 5.

3 Lay out the sashing rows and block rows in alternating positions, and sew the rows together. The pieced quilt center should now measure 58½" square, including seam allowances.

4 Sew together five green B 2½" squares and four cream 2½" × 12½" rectangles in alternating positions. Repeat for a total of four pieced sashing strips.

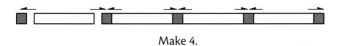

Make 4.

5 Join pieced sashing strips to the sides of the quilt top. Press the seam allowances away from the quilt center. Join a cream 2½" square to each end of the remaining sashing strips. Press the seam allowances toward the green print. Sew these strips to the top and bottom of the quilt top. Press the seam allowances away from the quilt center. The quilt top should now measure 62½" square.

## Finishing the Quilt

Refer to "Finishing Techniques" on page 236 for details on the following steps.

1 Layer and baste your quilt, and quilt as desired.

2 Using the remaining green A 2½"-wide strips, prepare and attach the binding.

Quilt assembly

# Blooming Stars

**FINISHED QUILT:** 62" × 62" • **FINISHED BLOCK:** 14" × 14"

*Designed and pieced by Deanne Eisenman; quilted by Annette Ashbach*
*of The Quiltmaker's Nest*

*This lap quilt is perfect for precut 2½"-wide strips, or raid your stash and cut strips from an assortment of your favorite colors. You'll need a total of at least two yards of fabric, drawing from as few or as many reproduction prints as you wish.*

## Materials

*Yardage is based on 42"-wide fabric. Fat quarters are 18" × 21".*

23 strips, 2½" × 42", OR ½ yard *each* of 4 assorted medium prints for blocks*

13 fat quarters OR 2⅞ yards *total* of assorted tan prints for blocks

6 fat quarters OR 1¼ yards *total* of assorted brown prints for blocks

1 yard of medium blue print for border

½ yard of medium red print for binding

3¾ yards of fabric for backing

70" × 70" piece of batting

*Cut each ½ yard of fabric into 6 strips, 2½" × 42" (1 is extra).*

## Cutting

*All measurements include ¼"-wide seam allowances. The pieces in this block are labeled A through G. When cutting pieces for the blocks, you'll want to cut the amount needed from various fabrics to achieve the desired scrappy look. For example, you would not want to cut all of the A pieces from the same strips of fabric.*

**From the assorted medium prints, cut a *total* of:**
64 rectangles, 2½" × 6½" (E)
64 rectangles, 2½" × 4½" (A)
64 squares, 2½" × 2½" (B)

**From the assorted tan prints, cut a *total* of:**
64 squares, 4½" × 4½" (F)
64 rectangles, 2½" × 4½" (D)
208 squares, 2½" × 2½" (C)

**From the assorted brown prints, cut a *total* of:**
64 squares, 4½" × 4½" (G)

**From the medium blue print, cut:**
8 strips, 3¼" × 42"

**From the medium red print, cut:**
7 strips, 2" × 42"

## Making the Units

Press the seam allowances as indicated by the arrows, or as otherwise instructed.

1  Draw a diagonal line from corner to corner on the wrong side of 128 tan C squares. Place a marked square on one end of a medium E rectangle, right sides together and corners aligned. Make sure the drawn line is positioned as shown. Sew on the line. Trim the excess fabric, leaving ¼" seam allowances, and press. Make a total of 64 E/C units.

Make 64.

2  Place a marked C square from step 1 on one end of a medium A rectangle, right sides together and with the drawn line positioned as shown. Sew on the line. Trim the excess fabric, leaving ¼" seam allowances, and press. Make a total of 64 A/C units.

Make 64.

**3** Draw a diagonal line from corner to corner on the wrong side of the medium B squares. Place a marked square on one end of a tan D rectangle, right sides together and with the drawn line positioned as shown. Sew on the line. Trim the excess fabric, leaving ¼" seam allowances, and press. Make a total of 64 D/B units.

Make 64.

**4** Join a tan C square to the top of an A/C unit as shown. Make 64.

Make 64.

**5** Join a tan F square to the top of a D/B unit as shown. Make 64.

Make 64.

**6** Join a unit from step 4 to a unit from step 5 as shown to make a corner unit. The unit should measure 6½" square, including seam allowances. Make a total of 64 units.

Make 64.

## Assembling the Blocks

**1** Sew two corner units from step 6 to opposite sides of an E/C unit as shown, rotating the corner units as needed so that the star points are directed away from the E/C unit. Make 32.

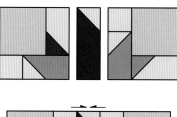

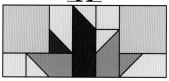

Make 32.

**2** Sew E/C units to opposite sides of a tan C square as shown. Make 16.

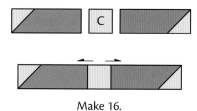

Make 16.

**3** Lay out two units from step 1 and one unit from step 2, making sure the units are facing in the direction shown. Sew the units together to make a block. The block should measure 14½" square, including seam allowances. Make 16 blocks.

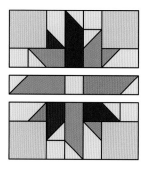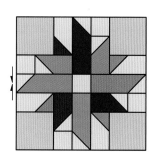

Make 16.

**4** Draw a diagonal line from corner to corner on the wrong side of the brown G squares. Place a marked square on the upper-right corner of a block as shown, right sides together and corners aligned. Sew on the drawn line. Trim the excess fabric, leaving ¼" seam allowances, and press. Repeat, adding brown squares to the remaining three corners of the block. Make a total of 16 Blooming Star blocks.

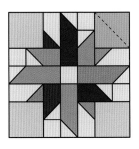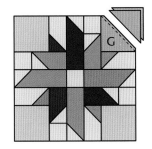

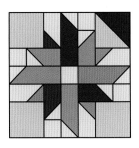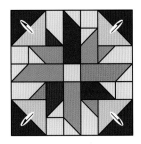

Make 16.

## Assembling the Quilt Top

1 Lay out the Blooming Star blocks in four rows of four blocks each.

2 Sew the blocks together into rows, and press the seam allowances in opposite directions from row to row. Sew the rows together and press the seam allowances in one direction.

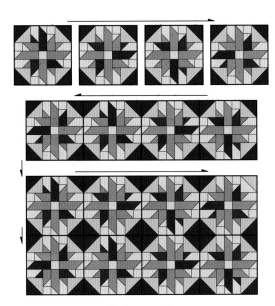

Quilt assembly

3 Measure the length of the quilt top through the center; it should be 56½". Trim four of the medium blue strips to 28½" long. Join the strips in pairs along the short ends to make two 56½"-long strips, and sew them to the sides of the quilt top. Measure the width of the quilt top through the center, including the borders just added; it should be 62". Trim the remaining medium blue strips to 31¼" long. Join the strips in pairs along the short ends to make two 62"-long strips, and sew them to the top and bottom of the quilt top.

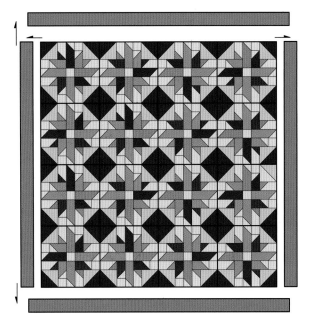

Adding borders

## Finishing the Quilt

Refer to "Finishing Techniques" on page 236 for details on the following steps.

1 Layer and baste your quilt, and quilt as desired.

2 Using the medium red 2"-wide strips, prepare and attach the binding.

*Blooming Stars*

# Shoofly Doll Quilt

**FINISHED QUILT:** 22" × 27½" • **FINISHED BLOCK:** 4½" × 4½"

*Designed and made by Kathleen Tracy*

*A shoofly was a child's rocker first made in the 1860s, with side supports that represented an animal figure. This little quilt treasure was inspired by imagining Civil War wives quilting or rocking in their own chairs, comforted by watching their children at play.*

## Materials

*Yardage is based on 42"-wide fabric.*

⅜ yard *total* of 6 assorted light prints for blocks*

¼ yard *total* of 6 assorted pink prints for blocks and border corner squares*

¼ yard *total* of 6 assorted brown prints for blocks and sashing squares*

¼ yard of pink floral for sashing

⅓ yard of dark brown print for border

¼ yard of dark pink print for binding

¾ yard of fabric for backing

26" × 32" piece of batting

*In the quilt shown, Kathleen went for a super-scrappy look by using slightly more or fewer prints. Feel free to follow her example, paying attention to the cutting quantities in parentheses for the total number of pieces needed.*

## Cutting

*All measurements include ¼"-wide seam allowances.*

**From *each* of the 6 assorted light prints, cut:**

4 squares, 2⅜" × 2⅜" (24 total)

8 squares, 2" × 2" (48 total)

**From *each* of the 6 assorted pink prints, cut:**

2 squares, 2⅜" × 2⅜" (12 total)

1 square, 2" × 2" (6 total)

**From *1* of the assorted pink prints, cut:**

4 squares, 3½" × 3½"

**From *each* of the 6 assorted brown prints, cut:**

2 squares, 2⅜" × 2⅜" (12 total)

1 square, 2" × 2" (6 total)

**From *1* of the assorted brown prints, cut:**

6 squares, 1½" × 1½"

**From the pink floral, cut:**

3 strips, 1½" × 42"; crosscut into 17 rectangles, 1½" × 5"

**From the dark brown print, cut:**

2 strips, 3½" × 42"; crosscut each strip into:
- 1 strip, 3½" × 16" (2 total)
- 1 strip, 3½" × 21½" (2 total)

**From the dark pink print, cut:**

3 strips, 1¼" × 42"

## Making the Blocks

Press the seam allowances as indicated by the arrows, or as otherwise instructed. The instructions are written for making one Shoofly block at a time.

1. Layer two matching light 2⅜" squares on top of two matching pink 2⅜" squares, right sides together. Draw a diagonal line from corner to corner on the wrong side of each light square. Stitch ¼" from the line on both sides and cut on the drawn line. Press the seam allowances toward the pink print. Make four half-square-triangle units.

Make 4.

2. Arrange the four units from step 1, a matching pink 2" square, and four matching light 2" squares in rows as shown on page 32. Sew the pieces into rows and press. Join the rows and press the seam

allowances away from the center. Make a total of six pink blocks and six brown blocks.

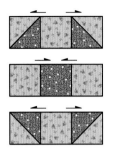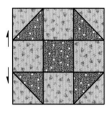

Make 6 pink blocks and 6 brown blocks.

## Assembling the Quilt Top

1 Sew three blocks together with two pink floral 1½" × 5" rectangles to make a row, alternating pink and brown blocks. Make four rows, two with pink blocks on the outside and two with brown blocks on the outside.

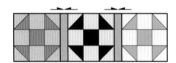

Make 4.

2 Sew three pink floral 1½" × 5" rectangles together with two brown 1½" squares to make a sashing row. Make three.

Make 3.

3 Sew the block rows and sashing rows together as shown.

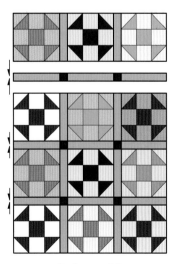

Quilt assembly

4 Sew the brown 3½" × 21½" strips to the sides of the quilt top. Sew a pink 3½" square to each end of the brown 3½" × 16" strips. Sew these strips to the top and bottom of the quilt top and press the seam allowances toward the borders.

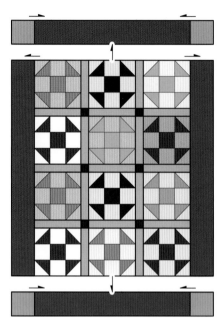

Adding borders

## Finishing the Quilt

Refer to "Finishing Techniques" on page 236 for details on the following steps.

1 Layer and baste your quilt, and quilt as desired.

2 Using the dark pink 1¼"-wide strips and referring to "Single-Fold Binding" on page 239, prepare and attach the binding.

# Miss Mary's Pinwheels

**FINISHED QUILT:** 33⅜" × 33⅜" • **FINISHED BLOCK:** 3½" × 3½"

*Designed and made by Carol Hopkins*

*Carol Hopkins created this quilt during a sewing retreat at Miss Mary's Quilting Cottage in Lafayette, Indiana. Because the pinwheels formed by the light triangles attract the vision more than the dark triangles, select light prints in a variety of eye-catching designs.*

## Materials

*Yardage is based on 42"-wide fabric.*

25 scraps, at least 3" × 6" each, of assorted dark prints for Pinwheel blocks

25 scraps, at least 3" × 6" each, of assorted light prints for Pinwheel blocks

1 yard of blue print for sashing, border, and binding

1⅓ yards of brown stripe OR ⅜ yard of nondirectional brown print for sashing

⅜ yard of olive-green print for setting triangles

1¼ yards of fabric for backing

38" × 38" piece of batting

## Cutting

*All measurements include ¼"-wide seam allowances.*

**From *each* of the 25 assorted dark prints, cut:**

2 squares, 2⅝" × 2⅝"; cut the squares in half diagonally to yield 4 triangles (100 total)

**From *each* of the 25 assorted light prints, cut:**

2 squares, 2⅝" × 2⅝"; cut the squares in half diagonally to yield 4 triangles (100 total)

**From the blue print, cut:**

4 strips, 3½" × 42"

32 rectangles, 1¾" × 4"

4 strips, 2" × 42"

**From the brown stripe, cut on the *lengthwise* grain:**

2 strips, 1¾" × 36"

2 strips, 1¾" × 28"

2 strips, 1¾" × 18"

2 strips, 1¾" × 8"

**From the olive-green print, cut:**

3 squares, 6¾" × 6¾"; cut the squares into quarters diagonally to yield 12 triangles

2 squares, 4" × 4"; cut the squares in half diagonally to yield 4 triangles

## Making the Blocks

Press the seam allowances as indicated by the arrows, or as otherwise instructed.

1 For each Pinwheel block, select four matching dark triangles and four matching light triangles. Sew the dark and light triangles together to make half-square-triangle units. Make four matching half-square-triangle units for each block (100 total). The units should measure 2¼" square, including seam allowances.

Make 4
matching units
(100 total).

2 Lay out four matching half-square-triangle units as shown. Sew the units together in rows, and then sew the rows together to make a Pinwheel block. Repeat to make a total of 25 Pinwheel blocks measuring 4" square, including seam allowances.

Make 25.

## Assembling the Quilt Top

1 Arrange the Pinwheel blocks, blue sashing rectangles, brown sashing strips, and olive-green side and corner triangles as shown. The striped sashing strips are longer than the block rows; center the strips between the rows of blocks so that you have equal amounts on each end. Do not trim the excess from the strips yet.

2 Sew the blocks, sashing rectangles, and side triangles into rows as shown. Sew the block rows and brown sashing strips together, and then add the corner triangles.

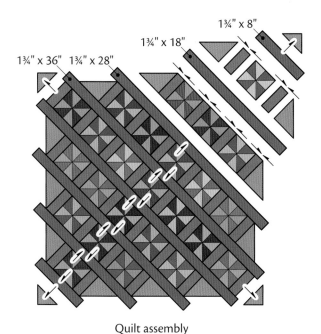

Quilt assembly

3 Trim and square up the quilt top, leaving 1" beyond the points of all the Pinwheel blocks.

4 Measure the length of the quilt top through the center and cut two blue 3½"-wide strips to this measurement. Sew the strips to the sides of the quilt top. Measure the width of the quilt top through the center, including the borders just added, and cut the remaining blue 3½"-wide strips to this measurement. Sew the strips to the top and bottom of the quilt top.

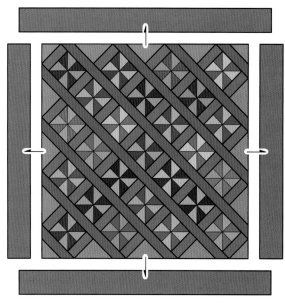

Adding borders

## Finishing the Quilt

Refer to "Finishing Techniques" on page 236 for details on the following steps.

1 Layer and baste your quilt, and quilt as desired.

2 Using the blue 2"-wide strips, prepare and attach the binding.

# Wheatland

**FINISHED QUILT:** 82" × 90½" • **FINISHED BLOCK:** 6" × 6"

*Designed by Paula Barnes; pieced by Mary Ellen Robison; quilted by Sharon Dixon*

*Wheatland, a Federal-style brick house in Lancaster County, Pennsylvania, was the final home of President James Buchanan, who left office in 1861 as the country teetered on the brink of the Civil War. Simple Checkerboard blocks look dynamic when paired with alternate blocks of large half-square triangles.*

## Materials

*Yardage is based on 42"-wide fabric.*

28 assorted dark prints, ⅛ yard each, for blocks

8 assorted light prints, ¼ yard each, for blocks

1½ yards of cheddar print A for blocks

1⅓ yards of tan print for pieced setting blocks and triangles

3¾ yards of navy print for pieced setting blocks, setting triangles, and fourth border

⅔ yard of cheddar print B for first and third borders

⅝ yard of medium brown print for second border

1 yard of fabric for binding

7½ yards of fabric for backing

90" × 99" piece of batting

## Cutting

*All measurements include ¼"-wide seam allowances. Do not cut the lengthwise border strips from the navy print until the quilt center is complete and you have determined the final measurements.*

**From *each* of the 28 assorted dark prints, cut:**

6 rectangles, 1½" × 7" (168 total)

**From *each* of the 8 assorted light prints, cut:**

3 strips, 1½" × 42"; crosscut into 14 rectangles, 1½" × 7" (112 total)

**From cheddar print A, cut:**

6 strips, 4½" × 42"; crosscut into 28 rectangles, 4½" × 7"

14 strips, 1½" × 42"; crosscut into 112 rectangles, 1½" × 4½"

**From the tan print, cut:**

5 strips, 7" × 42"; crosscut into 21 squares, 7" × 7"

1 strip, 5⅛" × 42"; crosscut into 6 squares, 5⅛" × 5⅛". Cut the squares in half diagonally to yield 12 triangles.

**From the navy print, cut:**

4 strips, 7" × 42"; crosscut into 20 squares, 7" × 7"*

1 strip, 9¾" × 42"; crosscut into 4 squares, 9¾" × 9¾". Cut the squares into quarters diagonally to yield 16 triangles (2 are extra).

**From the remainder of the navy print, cut on the *lengthwise* grain:**

2 strips, 7½" × 76¼"

2 strips, 7½" × 82"

1 square, 7" × 7"*

8 squares, 5⅛" × 5⅛"; cut the squares in half diagonally to yield 16 triangles

**From cheddar print B, cut:**

14 strips, 1½" × 42"

**From the medium brown print, cut:**

7 strips, 2½" × 42"

**From the binding fabric, cut:**

10 strips, 1⅞" × 42", or bias strips to total 380"

*\*You'll need a total of 21 squares. If you can cut them from the first 4 navy strips, you won't need to cut the additional square.*

# Making the Checkerboard Blocks

Press the seam allowances as indicated by the arrows, or as otherwise instructed.

1. Sew two matching dark 1½" × 7" rectangles and one cheddar A 4½" × 7" rectangle together to make a strip set. Cut four segments, 1½" wide. Make 28 strip sets and cut a total of 112 segments.

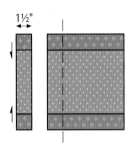

1½"

Make 28 strip sets.
Cut 112 segments.

2. Sew two matching dark 1½" × 7" rectangles and two matching light 1½" × 7" rectangles together. Cut four segments, 1½" wide.

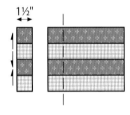

1½"

Cut 4 segments.

3. Sew the four segments from step 2 together as shown.

4. Repeat steps 2 and 3 to make a total of 56 checkerboard units.

5. Sew cheddar A 1½" × 4½" rectangles to opposite sides of a checkerboard unit. Add matching segments from step 1 to the top and bottom. Make a total of 56 blocks.

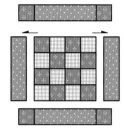 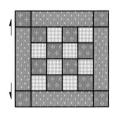

Make 56.

# Making the Alternate Blocks

Draw a diagonal line from corner to corner on the wrong side of the tan 7" squares. Place a marked square on a navy 7" square, right sides together and raw edges aligned. Stitch ¼" from the line on both sides and cut on the drawn line. Trim the two resulting half-square-triangle units to 6½" square, including seam allowances. Make 42 half-square-triangle units.

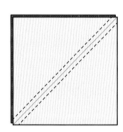 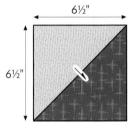

6½"

6½"

Make 42.

# Making the Pieced Setting Triangles

Sew a tan 5⅛" triangle together with a navy 5⅛" triangle as shown. Make six of each.

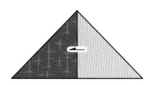 

Make 6 of each.

## Assembling the Quilt Top

1  Lay out the blocks in diagonal rows as shown, with seven blocks across and eight blocks down. Add the setting blocks and triangles to the layout, referring to the quilt assembly diagram for correct orientation. Rearrange the checkerboard blocks until you are pleased with the color placement.

2  Sew the pieces together into rows, and then join the rows. Add the corner triangles last.

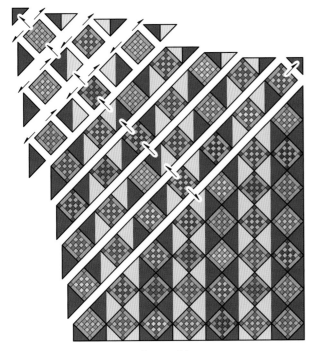

Quilt assembly

3  For the first border, trim the selvages from the cheddar B 1½" × 42" strips and sew the strips together end to end. Press the seam allowances to one side. From this strip cut two strips, 68⅜" long, for the side borders and two strips, 62" long, for the top and bottom borders. Attach the side borders first and then add the top and bottom borders. Set aside the remainder of the pieced strip for the third border.

4  For the second border, trim the selvages from the brown 2½" × 42" strips and sew the strips together end to end. Press the seam allowances to one side. From this strip cut two strips, 70¼" long, for the side borders and two strips, 66" long, for the top and bottom borders. Attach the side borders first and then add the top and bottom borders.

5  For the third border, cut the remaining pieced cheddar strip into two strips, 74¼" long, for the side borders and two strips, 68" long, for the top and bottom borders. Attach the side borders first and then add the top and bottom borders.

6  For the fourth border, attach the navy 7½" × 76¼" strips to the sides of the quilt top, and then add the navy 7½" × 82" strips to the top and bottom.

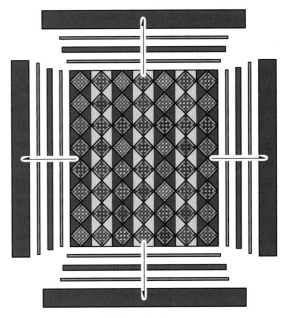

Adding borders

## Finishing the Quilt

Refer to "Finishing Techniques" on page 236 for details on the following steps.

1  Layer and baste your quilt, and quilt as desired.

2  Using the 1⅞"-wide binding strips, prepare and attach the binding.

# Path of Freedom

**FINISHED QUILT:** 36½" × 36½" • **FINISHED BLOCK:** 6" × 6"

*Designed and made by Mary Etherington and Connie Tesene*

*The Underground Railroad system helped shelter runaway slaves from the South and guide them on their journey northward. As more slaves gained their freedom in the mid-1800s, many worked to help others in the years leading up to the end of the Civil War and the abolition of slavery.*

## Materials

*Yardage is based on 42"-wide fabric.*
4 assorted red prints, ⅓ yard each, for Star blocks
4 assorted light prints, ⅓ yard each, for Star blocks and Double X blocks
⅛ yard of white print for Star block centers
⅛ yard of cream print for Double X blocks
4 assorted navy prints, ⅛ yard each, for Double X blocks
4 assorted gold prints, ⅛ yard each, for Double X blocks
⅓ yard of blue print for binding
1¼ yards of fabric for backing
40" × 40" piece of batting

## Cutting

*All measurements include ¼"-wide seam allowances.*

**From *each* of the 4 assorted red prints, cut:**
2 strips, 2" × 42"; crosscut into 40 squares, 2" × 2" (160 total)
4 squares, 3½" × 3½" (16 total)

**From *each of 3* light prints, cut:**
1 strip, 3½" × 42"; crosscut into 20 rectangles, 2" × 3½" (60 total)
1 strip, 2" × 42"; crosscut into 20 squares, 2" × 2" (60 total)
1 strip, 2⅞" × 42"; crosscut into 12 squares, 2⅞" × 2⅞". Cut the squares in half diagonally to yield 24 triangles (72 total).

**From *1* of the light prints, cut:**
1 strip, 3½" × 42"; crosscut into 20 rectangles, 2" × 3½"
1 strip, 2" × 42"; crosscut into 20 squares, 2" × 2"

**From the white print, cut:**
4 squares, 3½" × 3½"

**From the cream print, cut:**
1 strip, 2⅞" × 42"; crosscut into 12 squares, 2⅞" × 2⅞". Cut the squares in half diagonally to yield 24 triangles.

**From *each* of the 4 assorted navy prints, cut:**
1 strip, 2⅞" × 42"; crosscut into 12 squares, 2⅞" × 2⅞". Cut the squares in half diagonally to yield 24 triangles (96 total).

**From *each* of the 4 assorted gold prints, cut:**
1 strip, 2⅞" × 42"; crosscut into 12 squares, 2⅞" × 2⅞". Cut the squares in half diagonally to yield 24 triangles (96 total).

**From the blue print, cut:**
4 strips, 2¼" × 42"

# Making the Star Blocks

Use one light and one red print for each block. Press the seam allowances as indicated by the arrows, or as otherwise instructed.

1 Draw a diagonal line on the wrong side of each red 2" square. Place a marked square on one end of a light rectangle, right sides together and corners aligned. Sew on the drawn line. Trim the excess fabric of the red square only, ¼" from the stitched line, and press. Repeat on the other end of the rectangle. Make four units.

Make 4.

2 Lay out the units from step 1, four light 2" squares, and one red 3½" square in three rows as shown. Sew the pieces together into rows, and then join the rows. The block should measure 6½" square, including seam allowances. Make 16 blocks.

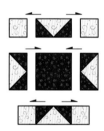 

Make 16.

3 Referring to steps 1 and 2, make four blocks using one light print, one red print, and the white squares as shown.

Make 4.

# Making the Double X Blocks

Use one light (or cream), one navy, and one gold print for each block.

1 Sew a light triangle to a navy triangle to make a half-square-triangle unit. Make three units.

Make 3.

2 Sew a light triangle to a gold triangle to make a half-square-triangle unit. Make three units.

Make 3.

3 Sew a gold triangle to a navy triangle to make a half-square-triangle unit. Make three units.

Make 3.

4 Join the units from steps 1–3 into rows, and then join the rows. The block should measure 6½" square, including seam allowances. Make 16 blocks.

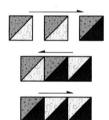 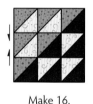

Make 16.

## Assembling the Quilt Top

1 Lay out the blocks in six rows of six blocks each, alternating the block designs and rotating the Double X blocks to form a gold diamond pattern in the quilt center as shown in the quilt assembly diagram.

2 Sew the blocks together into rows, and then join the rows.

## Finishing the Quilt

Refer to "Finishing Techniques" on page 236 for details on the following steps.

1 Layer and baste your quilt, and quilt as desired.

2 Using the blue 2¼"-wide strips, prepare and attach the binding.

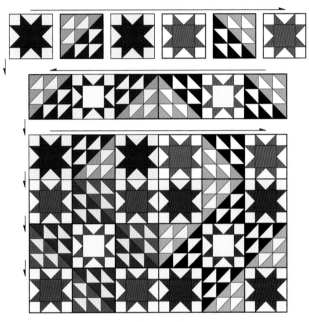

Quilt assembly

# Paint the Sky

**FINISHED QUILT:** 65½" × 85½" • **FINISHED BLOCK:** 5" × 5"

*Designed and pieced by Laurie Baker; quilted by Sherrie Coppenbarger*

*Camping out can be fun (even indoors) when you sleep under the restful stars of this scrappy bed-sized quilt. All you need is the nighttime singing of frogs and crickets to lull you into a peaceful slumber.*

## Materials

*Yardage is based on 42"-wide fabric.*

1⅝ yards *total* of assorted medium and dark prints for stars

4⅝ yards *total* of assorted light prints for background

1⅓ yards of red print for inner border and binding

2½ yards of tan print for outer border

5⅝ yards of fabric for backing

72" × 92" piece of batting

## Cutting

*All measurements include ¼"-wide seam allowances.*

**From the assorted medium and dark prints, cut a *total* of:**

60 squares, 3⅜" × 3⅜"; cut the squares in half diagonally to yield 120 triangles

120 squares, 3" × 3"

**From the assorted light prints, cut a *total* of:**

16 squares, 10½" × 10½"

8 rectangles, 5½" × 10½"

64 rectangles, 3" × 10½"

12 rectangles, 3" × 5½"

**From the red print, cut:**

7 strips, 3" × 42"

8 strips, 2½" × 42"

**From the tan print, cut on the *lengthwise* grain:**

2 strips, 3" × 80½"

2 strips, 3" × 65½"

## Making the Blocks

Press the seam allowances as indicated by the arrows, or as otherwise instructed.

1. Randomly select two medium or dark 3⅜" triangles and join them along the long bias edges. Trim away the dog-ear points. Repeat to make a total of 60 half-square-triangle units.

Make 60.

2. Lay out four half-square-triangle units in two rows of two units each, making sure the seams are positioned as shown. Sew the units in each row together, and then join the rows. Repeat to make a total of 15 blocks measuring 5½" square, including seam allowances.

Make 15.

## Making the Sashing and Border Units

1. Draw a diagonal line on the wrong side of each medium or dark 3" square. Place a marked square on one end of a light 3" × 10½" rectangle, right sides together and corners aligned. Sew on the drawn line. Trim the excess fabric, leaving ¼" seam allowances, and press. Repeat for a total of 32 units and 32 mirror-image units.

Make 32 of each.

2 Sew one of each unit from step 1 together as shown to make a long single-point unit. Repeat to make a total of 10 units.

Make 10.

3 Using a prepared medium or dark square, create a corner triangle on the opposite end of each remaining unit from step 1 as shown. Sew one of each unit together to make a double-point unit. Repeat to make a total of 22 units.

Make 22 of each.    Make 22 total.

4 Using a prepared medium or dark square, create a corner triangle on each light 3" × 5½" rectangle to make six units and six mirror-image units. Sew one of each unit together as shown to make a short single-point unit. Repeat to make a total of six units.

Make 6 of each.    Make 6 total.

## Assembling the Quilt Top

1 Lay out three blocks, two long single-point units, and two double-point units as shown to form row A. Sew the pieces together. Repeat to make a total of five A rows.

Row A.
Make 5.

2 Lay out four assorted light 10½" squares and three double-point units as shown to form row B. Sew the pieces together. Repeat to make a total of four B rows.

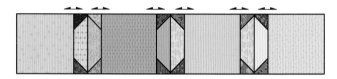

Row B.
Make 4.

3 Lay out four assorted light 5½" × 10½" rectangles and three short single-point units as shown to make row C. Sew the pieces together. Repeat to make a total of two C rows.

Row C.
Make 2.

4 Refer to the quilt assembly diagram at right to lay out the A and B rows in alternating positions. Join the rows. Press the seam allowances open. Add the C rows to the top and bottom of the pieced unit as shown. Press the seam allowances open. The quilt top should measure 55½" × 75½", including seam allowances.

5 Sew the red 3" × 42" strips together end to end to make one long strip. From this pieced strip, cut two strips, 75½" long, and join them to the sides of the quilt top. From the remainder of the pieced strip, cut two strips, 60½" long, and join them to the top and bottom of the quilt top.

6 Sew the tan 3" × 80½" strips to the sides of the quilt top, and then sew the tan 3" × 65½" strips to the top and bottom.

## Finishing the Quilt

Refer to "Finishing Techniques" on page 236 for details on the following steps.

1 Layer and baste your quilt, and quilt as desired.

2 Using the red 2½"-wide strips, prepare and attach the binding.

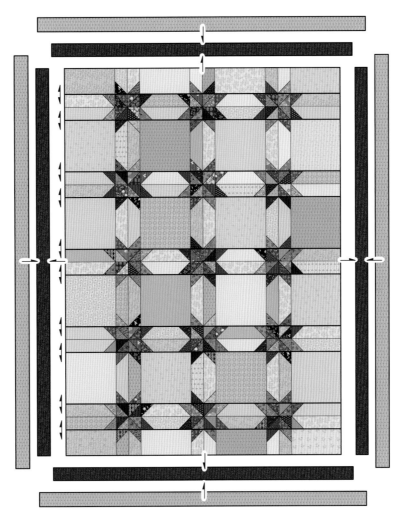

Quilt assembly

# Farmhouse Quilt

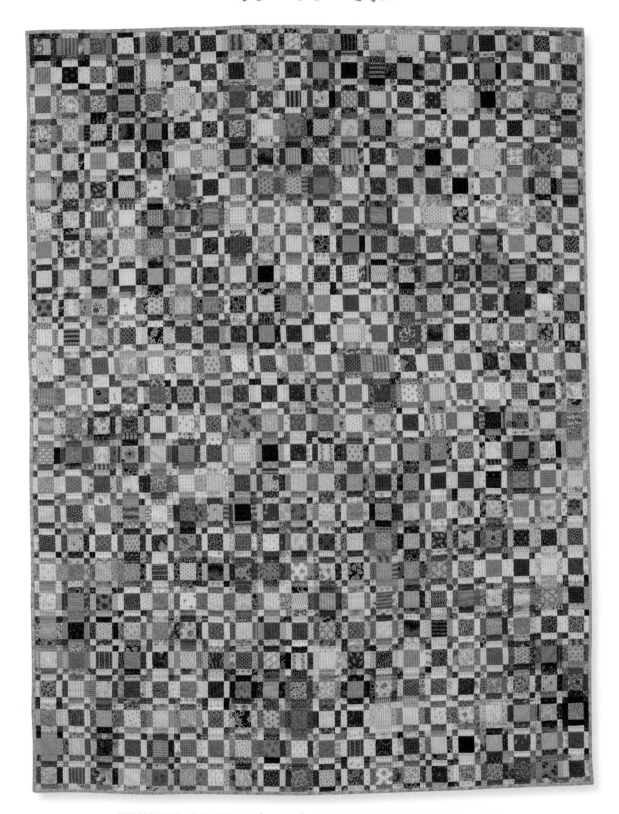

**FINISHED QUILT:** 70½" × 91½" • **FINISHED BLOCK:** 3½" × 3½"

*Designed and made by Mary Elizabeth Kinch and Biz Storms*

*Use the designers' clever assembly technique to pull this scrappy quilt together quickly and easily. With a wide variety of fabrics, colors, and value contrasts, you have the freedom to join the blocks into rows randomly without "art directing" as you sew.*

## Materials

*Yardage is based on 42"-wide fabric. While the yardage listed is total yardage needed, purchasing quarter yards, fat quarters (18" × 21"), and even fat eighths (9" × 21") will help you acquire the assortment of colors and values you'll need for this quilt.*

11 yards *total* of assorted brown, blue, light shirting, green, and purple prints for blocks*
⅞ yard of fabric for binding
5⅝ yards of fabric for backing
78" × 98" piece of batting

*The quilt shown contains a fabric mix of roughly 30% browns, 30% blues, 20% light shirtings, 15% purples, and 5% greens.*

## Cutting

*All measurements include ¼"-wide seam allowances. The designers loosely adhered to a strategy of using contrasting values for the corner squares and side rectangles of each block, and they also tried to cut each corner square and side rectangle in the block from a different fabric.*

**From the assorted brown, blue, light shirting, green, and purple prints, cut a *total* of:**
520 squares, 2½" × 2½"
2080 squares, 1¼" × 1¼"
2080 rectangles, 1¼" × 2½"

**From the binding fabric, cut:**
9 strips, 2¾" × 42"

## Making the Block Rows

The following construction technique is called the "batch-work method" by quilt designers Mary Elizabeth and Biz, and they enthusiastically promise that it is more fun than the usual assembly-line technique. They suggest trying to make a 26-block vertical row in a single sitting. Press the seam allowances as indicated by the arrows, or as otherwise instructed.

1 Randomly select 20 of the 2½" center squares and lay them out individually on a flat surface. Next, place a set of four 1¼" corner squares and then four 1¼" × 2½" side rectangles on top of each block center. Don't be too worried about adhering to any rules; just relax and deal out the fabrics like a deck of cards.

2 After selecting fabrics for the first 20 blocks, randomly deal out fabric pieces for the next 20 blocks, placing a set on top of each of your original stacks—no peeking allowed!

3 Continue making sets of pieces for 20 blocks, stacking a block on top of each of your previous stacks until all the pieces are gone. You will now have 20 stacks, each with enough fabric pieces to make 26 blocks—a vertical row.

4 Take one stack to your sewing machine and arrange the pieces for the first block. With right sides together, chain piece the pieces in the right-hand row to the pieces in the center row as shown. Do not cut the thread. Layer the remaining two corner squares and the side rectangle from the first block in sewing order (square, rectangle, square) and set them aside. They'll be added to the block after all 26 blocks in the batch have been partially assembled.

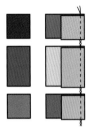 

5 Arrange the pieces for the next block in the stack and chain piece as described in step 4. Layer the remaining pieces and place them on top of the remaining pieces for block 1. Continue arranging, chain piecing, and layering until you have finished the last block in the stack. Cut the chain loose after sewing the last pair, *but do not cut the pairs apart.*

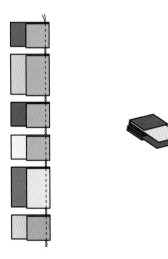

6 Rotate the chain so you are starting at the bottom of the row you finished in step 5. Working from the top of the stack of set-aside pieces, chain piece a corner square or side rectangle to the opposite edge of each unit on the chain as shown; press. Cut the chain loose after sewing the last units, *but do not cut the units apart.* Finger-press the units as shown.

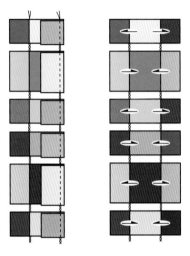

7 With right sides together, stitch the first, second, and third rows of the first block together as shown, carefully butting the seam allowances. Repeat to assemble the remaining blocks, stitching each to the previous block until the chain is complete. Trim any dangling threads and press the seam allowances in one direction. Label this row 1.

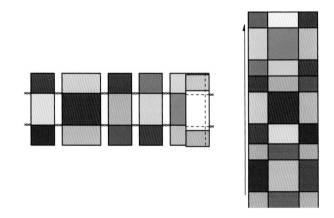

8 Repeat steps 4–7 to assemble the remaining 19 rows, labeling them row 2, row 3, and so on.

## Assembling the Quilt Top

1 Referring to the assembly diagram below, arrange the 20 vertical rows side by side.

2 With right sides together, join the vertical rows, carefully butting the seam allowances. Press the seam allowances in one direction.

## Finishing the Quilt

Refer to "Finishing Techniques" on page 236 for details on the following steps.

1 Layer and baste your quilt, and quilt as desired.

2 Using the 2¾"-wide binding strips, prepare and attach the binding.

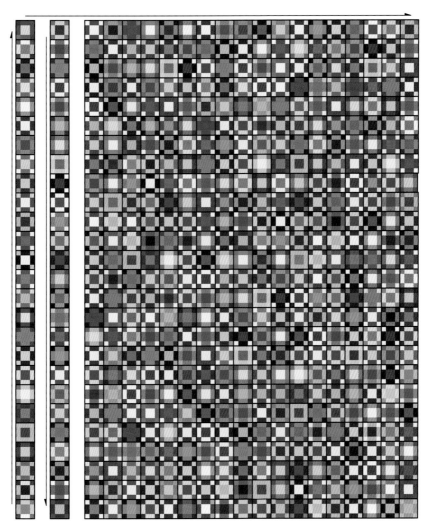

Quilt assembly

# Old-Time Treasures

**FINISHED QUILT:** 59" × 77" • **FINISHED BLOCK:** 8" × 8"

*Designed and made by Evelyn Sloppy*

*Lots of Civil War reproduction prints in warm browns and reds found their way into this diagonally set quilt. Packed with scraps, even in the setting triangles, but finished off without a border, it has a definite old-time feel.*

## Materials

*Yardage is based on 42"-wide fabric. Fat quarters are 18" × 21".*

3 yards *total* OR 12 fat quarters of assorted red and tangerine prints for blocks and sashing

3½ yards *total* OR 14 fat quarters of light and medium brown prints for blocks and setting triangles

2 yards *total* OR 8 fat quarters of dark brown prints for sashing

¾ yard of fabric for binding

4¾ yards of fabric for backing

63" × 81" piece of batting

## Cutting

*All measurements include ¼"-wide seam allowances.*

**From the red and tangerine prints, cut a *total* of:**
144 squares, 2½" × 2½"
48 strips, 2" × 18"
110 squares, 2" × 2"

**From the light and medium brown prints, cut a *total* of:**
144 rectangles, 2½" × 4½"
38 squares, 4½" × 4½"
12 squares, 8" × 8"; cut the squares into quarters diagonally to yield 48 triangles (2 are extra)

**From the dark brown prints, cut a *total* of:**
24 strips, 2" × 18"
31 squares, 5" × 5"

**From the binding fabric, cut:**
8 strips, 2½" × 42", or bias strips to total 295"

## Making the Blocks

Press the seam allowances as indicated by the arrows, or as otherwise instructed.

1. Draw a diagonal line from corner to corner on the wrong side of the red and tangerine 2½" squares. Place a marked square on one end of a light or medium brown 2½" × 4½" rectangle, right sides together and corners aligned. Sew on the line. Trim the excess fabric, leaving ¼" seam allowances, and press. Make 72 pointing to the left and 72 pointing to the right.

Make 72.                Make 72.

2. Sew together one of each unit from step 1 as shown. Repeat to make 72 units that measure 4½" square, including seam allowances.

Make 72.

3 Sew together four assorted units from step 2 to complete the block. Make 18 blocks that measure 8½" square, including seam allowances. To avoid bulk, you may prefer to press the final seam allowances open as you sew the units together.

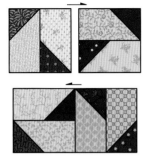 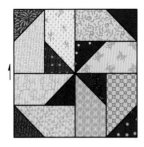

Make 18.

5" squares. Make 17 of these cornerstone units. Make another 14 units with marked squares added to just three corners. These units will be used on the edges of the quilt.

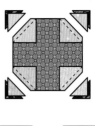

Make 17.          Make 14.

## Making the Sashing and Cornerstones

1 Sew together one dark brown and two red or tangerine 2"-wide strips along their long edges. Crosscut the strip set into 8½"-wide segments. Make a total of 24 strip sets and cut 48 segments for sashing units. They should measure 5" × 8½", including seam allowances.

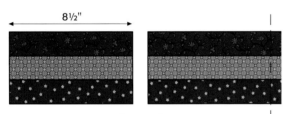

8½"

Make 24 strip sets.
Cut 48 segments.

2 Draw a diagonal line on the wrong side of the red and tangerine 2" squares. Referring to step 1 of "Making the Blocks" on page 53, sew marked squares to all four corners of the dark brown

## Making the Setting Triangles

1 Sew together three assorted light or medium brown 4½" squares and two triangles cut from the 8" squares to make the side setting triangles. Make six for the quilt sides and four for the top and bottom.

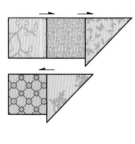 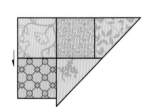

Make 6 side units.

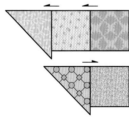 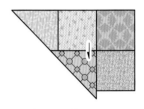

Make 4 top/bottom units.

2 Sew together two assorted light or medium brown 4½" squares and four triangles cut from the 8" squares to make the corner setting triangles. Make four.

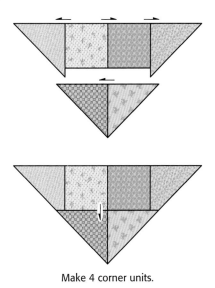

Make 4 corner units.

## Assembling the Quilt Top

1 Lay out the blocks, sashing units, cornerstone units, side setting triangles, and the remaining triangles cut from the light or medium brown 8" squares into diagonal rows. The edge triangles have been cut slightly oversized.

2 Sew the pieces together into rows, and then join the rows. Add the four corner units last.

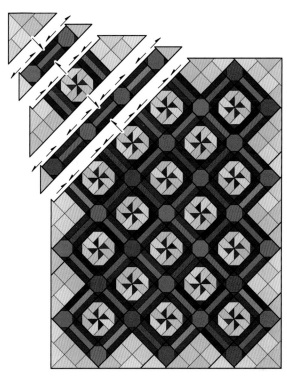

Quilt assembly

3 Trim the edges of the quilt top, leaving a ¼" seam allowance beyond the points of the blocks.

## Finishing the Quilt

Refer to "Finishing Techniques" on page 236 for details on the following steps.

1 Layer and baste your quilt, and quilt as desired.

2 To make the quilt with rounded corners as shown in the photo on page 52, simply trim the corners using a dinner plate as a guide. Then use 2½"-wide bias strips to prepare and attach the binding. If you would like to leave the corners of the quilt square, you can use 2½"-wide straight-grain strips to bind the quilt.

# Elizabeth's Baskets

**FINISHED QUILT:** 30⅝" × 36¼" • **FINISHED BLOCK:** 4" × 4"

*Designed and pieced by Carol Hopkins; quilted by Lisa Ramsey*

*This pattern is based on an unusual Basket block seen in an antique quilt. Using large-scale prints for some of the basket bases will break up the uniformity of the blocks and create movement across the quilt top.*

## Materials

*Yardage is based on 42"-wide fabric.*

½ yard of light print for blocks

20 scraps, at least 3" × 7" each, of assorted medium prints for blocks

20 scraps, at least 6" × 8" each, of assorted dark prints for blocks

⅝ yard of small-scale green print for setting squares and triangles

⅓ yard of black print for inner border

1⅜ yards of green directional print OR ¾ yard of green nondirectional print for outer border and binding

1¼ yards of fabric for backing

39" × 45" piece of batting

## Cutting

*All measurements include ¼"-wide seam allowances.*

**From the light print, cut:**

4 strips, 1½" × 42"; crosscut into:
- 40 rectangles, 1½" × 2½"
- 20 squares, 1½" × 1½"

3 strips, 1⅞" × 42"; crosscut into 50 squares, 1⅞" × 1⅞". Cut the squares in half diagonally to yield 100 triangles.

**From *each* of the 20 medium prints, cut:**

3 squares, 1⅞" × 1⅞"; cut the squares in half diagonally to yield 6 triangles (120 total)

**From *each* of the 20 dark prints, cut:**

1 square, 2⅞" × 2⅞"; cut the square in half diagonally to yield 2 triangles (40 total; 20 are extra)

3 squares, 1½" × 1½" (60 total)

1 square, 1⅞" × 1⅞"; cut the square in half diagonally to yield 2 triangles (40 total; 20 are extra)

**From the small-scale green print, cut:**

1 strip, 7" × 42"; cut into:
- 4 squares, 7" × 7"; cut the squares into quarters diagonally to yield 16 triangles (2 are extra)
- 2 squares, 3¾" × 3¾"; cut the squares in half diagonally to yield 4 triangles

2 strips, 4½" × 42"; crosscut into 12 squares, 4½" × 4½"

**From the black print, cut:**

4 strips, 1¼" × 42"

**From the green directional print, cut on the *crosswise* grain:\***

2 strips, 3½" × 42"

**From the remainder of the green directional print, cut on the *lengthwise* grain:\***

2 strips, 3½" × 38"

4 strips, 2" × 38"

*\*Cutting half of the outer-border strips crosswise and half of them lengthwise allows the directional motif to appear right side up all around the quilt. If you prefer to use ¾ yard of a nondirectional print, all of the strips can be cut on the crosswise grain. In that case, you'll need 4 strips, 3½" × 42", for the border and 4 strips, 2" × 42", for binding.*

# Making the Basket Blocks

The light print is paired with a different dark and medium print in each of the blocks. Instructions are for making one block. Press the seam allowances as indicated by the arrows, or as otherwise instructed.

1   Sew a dark 1⅞" triangle to a light 1⅞" triangle to make a half-square-triangle unit measuring 1½" square, including seam allowances.

Make 1.

2   Sew a medium 1⅞" triangle to a light 1⅞" triangle to make a half-square-triangle unit. Make four matching units measuring 1½" square, including seam allowances.

Make 4.

3   Sew the units from step 2 into pairs as shown.

4   Sew two medium 1⅞" triangles to a dark 1½" square. Trim off the dog-ear points.

Trim.

5   Sew the unit from step 4 to a matching dark 2⅞" triangle. Trim off the dog-ear points.

   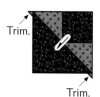

Trim.

Trim.

6   Arrange two light 1½" × 2½" rectangles, one light 1½" square, the units from steps 3 and 5, and two matching dark 1½" squares as shown. Sew the pieces together into rows, and then join the rows to make a block measuring 4½" square, including seam allowances. Make 20 blocks.

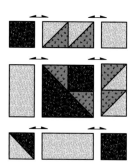   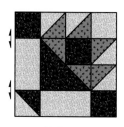

Make 20.

## Assembling the Quilt Top

1 Arrange the blocks, green 4½" squares, and green side and corner triangles in diagonal rows as shown in the assembly diagram below.

2 Sew the blocks, setting squares, and side triangles together in diagonal rows; press. Sew the rows together and press the seam allowances open. Add the green corner triangles; press.

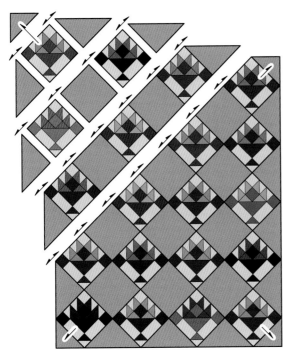

Quilt assembly

3 Trim the edges of the quilt top, leaving a ¼" seam allowance beyond the points of the blocks.

4 Measure the length of the quilt top through the center and trim two black 1¼"-wide strips to this measurement. Sew the strips to the sides of the quilt top. Measure the width of the quilt top through the center, including the borders just added, and trim the two remaining black strips to this measurement. Sew the strips to the top and bottom of the quilt top.

5 Measure the length of the quilt top through the center and trim the two 3½"-wide strips cut *lengthwise* from the green directional print to this measurement. Sew the strips to the sides of the quilt top. Measure the width of the quilt top through the center, including the borders just added, and trim the two 3½"-wide strips cut *crosswise* from the green directional print to this measurement. Sew the strips to the top and bottom of the quilt top.

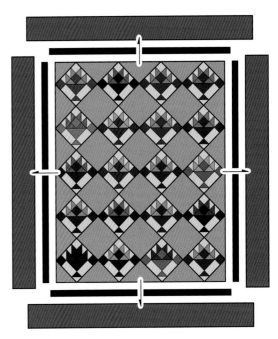

Adding borders

## Finishing the Quilt

Refer to "Finishing Techniques" on page 236 for details on the following steps.

1 Layer and baste your quilt, and quilt as desired.

2 Using the green 2"-wide strips, prepare and attach the binding.

# Fields of Valor

**FINISHED QUILT:** 44" × 44" • **FINISHED BLOCK:** 9" × 9"

*Designed and pieced by Carol Hopkins; quilted by Lisa Ramsey*

*Bold interplay of darks and lights brings to mind images of Civil War battles fought in fields divided by rail fences. Carol Hopkins dedicated this quilt to all soldiers who take risks and make personal sacrifices to serve their country.*

## Materials

*Yardage is based on 42"-wide fabric.*

9 scraps, at least 11" × 11" each, of assorted dark prints for blocks

9 scraps, at least 11" × 11" each, of assorted medium prints for blocks

9 scraps, at least 6" × 9" each, of assorted light prints for blocks

¼ yard of tan print for cornerstones

⅞ yard of gold print for sashing and binding

1⅜ yards of red print for border

3 yards of fabric for backing

52" × 52" piece of batting

## Cutting

*All measurements include ¼"-wide seam allowances.*

**From *each* of the 9 dark prints, cut:**

1 square, 3½" × 3½" (9 total)

4 squares, 2⅜" × 2⅜"; cut the squares in half diagonally to yield 8 triangles (72 total)

8 squares, 2" × 2" (72 total)

**From *each* of the 9 medium prints, cut:**

4 squares, 3½" × 3½" (36 total)

6 squares, 2⅜" × 2⅜"; cut the squares in half diagonally to yield 12 triangles (108 total)

**From *each* of the 9 light prints, cut:**

6 squares, 2⅜" × 2⅜"; cut the squares in half diagonally to yield 12 triangles (108 total)

**From the tan print, cut:**

16 squares, 2½" × 2½"

**From the gold print, cut:**

24 rectangles, 2½" × 9½"

5 strips, 2" × 42"

**From the red print, cut on the *lengthwise* grain:**

4 strips, 5" × 46"

## Making the Blocks

Combine a different light, medium, and dark print for each block. Instructions are for making one block. Press the seam allowances as indicated by the arrows, or as otherwise instructed.

1  Sew a dark triangle to a medium triangle to make a half-square-triangle unit measuring 2" square, including seam allowances. Make four.

2  Repeat step 1 using four dark and four light triangles to make four half-square-triangle units.

3  Repeat step 1 using eight medium and eight light triangles to make eight half-square-triangle units.

Make 4.   Make 4.

Make 8.

4  Arrange the half-square-triangle units as shown. Sew the pieces together into rows, and then sew the rows together to make a corner unit. Make four corner units.

Make 4.

5  Position two dark 2" squares on adjacent corners of a medium 3½" square. Sew diagonally across the dark squares as shown to make a side unit. Make four matching units.

Make 4.

6 Arrange the corner and side units and a matching dark 3½" square in three rows as shown. Sew the pieces together into rows, and then join the rows to make a block measuring 9½" square, including seam allowances. Make nine blocks.

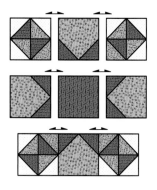 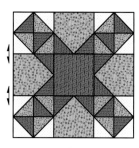

Make 9.

## Assembling the Quilt Top

1 Lay out the blocks in three rows of three blocks each, arranging them with the sashing rectangles and cornerstones as shown in the assembly diagram.

2 Sew the pieces together into rows, and then join the rows.

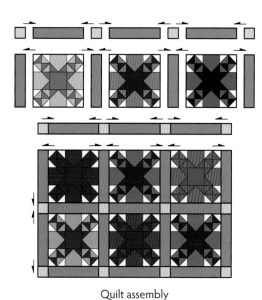

Quilt assembly

3 Measure the length of the quilt top through the center and trim two red 5"-wide strips to this measurement. Sew the strips to the sides of the quilt top. Measure the width of the quilt top through the center, including the borders just added, and trim the two remaining red strips to this measurement. Sew the strips to the top and bottom of the quilt top.

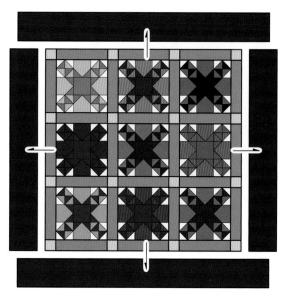

Adding borders

## Finishing the Quilt

Refer to "Finishing Techniques" on page 236 for details on the following steps.

1 Layer and baste your quilt, and quilt as desired.

2 Using the gold 2"-wide strips, prepare and attach the binding.

# Cabin Corners

**FINISHED QUILT:** 14¾" × 14¾" • **FINISHED BLOCK:** 4¾" × 4¾"

*Designed and made by Jo Morton*

*This little topper consists of just five Courthouse Steps blocks and four Log Cabin blocks, but you'll be amazed at how many scrappy prints you'll use. A red square sits at the heart of each block, echoing the deep values in the quilt corners.*

## Materials

*Yardage is based on 42"-wide fabric. Fat quarters are 18" × 21"; fat eighths are 9" × 21".*

1 fat eighth of red print for block centers

½ yard *total* of assorted light and medium prints for block logs

¼ yard *total* of assorted dark prints for block logs

1 fat quarter OR ¼ yard of rust print for binding

½ yard of fabric for backing

20" × 20" piece of batting

## Cutting

*All measurements include ¼"-wide seam allowances. Cut all of the logs from the lengthwise grain (parallel to the selvages), so that the blocks will lie flat. Crosswise strips have more stretch, making it more difficult to keep the blocks flat and smooth.*

*The number of strips you need for each dark and light print depends on the position of the strips in the block and how often the print is repeated. For each of the Log Cabin blocks, you'll need four dark and four light fabrics. For each of the Courthouse Steps blocks, you'll need four light or medium fabrics (one print for each round of logs). Start by cutting four strips of each print, and then cut more as needed.*

**From the red print, cut:**

9 squares, 1¼" × 1¼"

**From the assorted light and medium prints, cut on the *lengthwise* grain:**

36 strips, at least 1" × 12" or longer

**From the assorted dark prints, cut on the *lengthwise* grain:**

16 strips, at least 1" × 12" or longer

**From the rust print, cut:**

4 strips, 1⅛" × 21"

### DESIGN OPTION

You may like to make a runner of four or five blocks in a single row for an adorable accent piece. Another idea is to use a single block for a mug rug: With the block and backing right sides together, place the batting on top of the layers and sew around the outer edges leaving a small opening. Turn right side out, whipstitch the opening closed, and quilt a couple of rounds to hold the layers in place. What a nice gift for a sewing friend!

## Making the Log Cabin Blocks

Sew the strips or "logs" around the red center square in a clockwise manner, starting with light or medium strips on the first two adjacent sides and dark strips on the remaining two sides. Follow the numbered sequence in the block diagram on page 65 to sew the strips to a red 1¼" square. Use the same light or medium print for the first two strips, then switch to a dark print and use it for the next two positions. Continue using one light or medium and one dark print per round to make the block. Place the strip beneath the square or unit for sewing. It's important to use an accurate ¼"-wide seam allowance to ensure that all of the blocks finish to the same size. Press the seam allowances as indicated by the arrows, or as otherwise instructed.

1 Select four dark and four light or medium strips for each of the four Log Cabin blocks as follows.

**Round 1:**

light or medium print A for positions 1 and 2; dark print A for positions 3 and 4

**Round 2:**

light or medium print B for positions 5 and 6; dark print B for positions 7 and 8

**Round 3:**

light or medium print C for positions 9 and 10;
    dark print C for positions 11 and 12

**Round 4:**

light or medium print D for positions 13 and 14;
    dark print D for positions 15 and 16

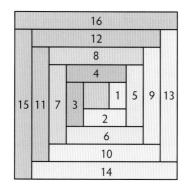

Log Cabin block

2 Sew a red 1¼" square to one end of a light or medium A strip, right sides together. Press to set the seam, and then press the seam allowances away from the red square (see "Press, Don't Iron" below right). Using a rotary cutter and mat and an acrylic ruler, trim the ends of the strip even with the red square.

3 Align the remainder of the light or medium A strip with the bottom edge of the unit from step 2, right sides together and at the end of the strip. Sew together; press to set the seam, and then press the seam allowances away from the square. Trim the strip ends even with the unit.

4 Align a dark A strip with the left side of the unit from step 3, right sides together. Sew, press, and trim as before.

5 Align the remainder of the dark A strip with the top of the unit from step 4, right sides together and at the end of the strip. Sew, press, and trim as before. You now have added logs to all four sides of the unit, completing round 1. Trim the unit as necessary to measure 2¼" square, including seam allowances.

6 Continue to add three additional rounds of dark and light or medium strips in clockwise rotation around the unit. Sew, press, and trim each strip as before. Trim as necessary to complete a Log Cabin block that measures 5¼" square, including seam allowances.

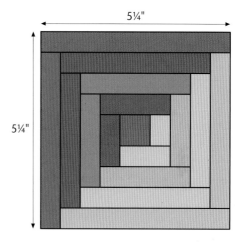

7 Repeat steps 2–6 to make a total of four Log Cabin blocks.

### PRESS, DON'T IRON

As you sew together the strips (logs) to assemble the blocks, first press to set the seam, and then press the strip away from the center. When you press, set the iron over the seam and lift it up; do not slide the iron across the seam or your seams may bow outward. Use your ruler and rotary cutter to trim the ends and keep the unit straight and square.

# Making the Courthouse Steps Blocks

Unlike a Log Cabin block, the logs in a Courthouse Steps block are added to opposite sides of the center square first, then added to the two remaining sides. In these blocks, each round of logs will use one light or medium strip for all four sides of the round. Follow the numbered sequence shown in the block diagram below to add the strips to a red 1¼" square. Place the strip beneath the square or unit for sewing. It's important to use an accurate ¼"-wide seam allowance to ensure that all of the blocks finish to the same size.

1 Select four light or medium strips for each of the five Courthouse Steps blocks as follows. Follow the numbered strips in the block diagram to make each Courthouse Steps block, placing each strip under the center square unit to sew them together.

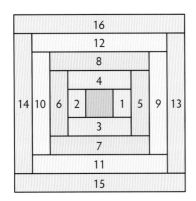

Courthouse Steps block

2 Sew a red 1¼" square to one end of a light or medium A strip, right sides together, with the square on top. Press to set the seam, and then press the seam allowances away from the red square. Using a rotary cutter and mat and an acrylic ruler, trim the ends of the light or medium strip even with the red square.

3 In the same manner, sew a matching light or medium A strip to the opposite side of the red square. Press and trim as before.

4 Sew a matching light or medium A strip to the top edge of the unit. Press and trim as before. Sew the remaining matching light or medium A strip to the bottom edge of the unit. Press and trim. You now have added one round of matching strips to four sides. Trim the unit to measure 2¼" square, including seam allowances.

   *Note:* Be careful when pressing that you do not distort the unit. Measure the unit after adding and pressing each round of strips, squaring the quilt top if needed to maintain accuracy. Each complete round of strips will add 1" to the measurement.

5 In the same manner, continue adding the light or medium strips in sequence to opposite sides of the unit to make a Courthouse Steps block. Sew, press, and trim each strip as before. The block should measure 5¼" square, including seam allowances.

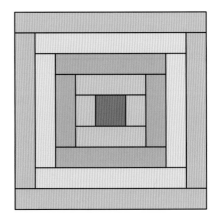

6 Repeat steps 2–5 to make a total of five Courthouse Steps blocks.

## Assembling the Quilt Top

1 Arrange the Log Cabin and Courthouse Steps blocks in three rows of three blocks each, rotating the Log Cabin blocks so that the dark prints are on the outer edges of the quilt top.

2 Sew the blocks together into rows, and then join the rows.

## Finishing the Quilt

Refer to "Finishing Techniques" on page 236 for details on the following steps.

1 Layer and baste your quilt, and quilt as desired.

2 Using the rust 1⅛"-wide strips and referring to "Single-Fold Binding" on page 239, prepare and attach the binding.

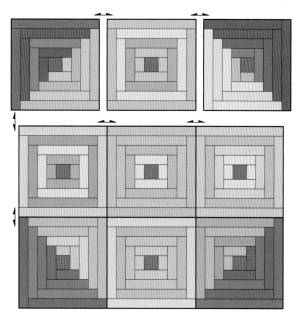

Quilt assembly

# Stars over Mitford

**FINISHED QUILT:** 71" × 95" • **FINISHED BLOCK:** 12" × 12"

*Designed and made by Pat Speth*

*Just like the stars in the sky, the stars in this design are there—you just don't always see them. Made with a multitude of reproduction fabrics, this quilt provides a great exercise in the placement of dark and medium values within a block.*

## Materials

*Yardage is based on 42"-wide fabric.*

105 different pairs of squares, 5" × 5", of assorted dark and medium prints for blocks

35 squares, 5" × 5", of assorted dark and medium prints for blocks

70 different pairs of squares, 5" × 5", of assorted light prints for blocks

35 squares, 5" × 5", of assorted light prints for blocks

½ yard of medium print for inner border

2⅛ yards of dark print for outer border and binding

5⅞ yards of fabric for backing

77" × 101" piece of batting

## Cutting

*All measurements include ¼"-wide seam allowances.*

**From the medium print for inner border, cut:**
8 strips, 1½" × 42"

**From the dark print for outer border and binding, cut:**
9 strips, 4¾" × 42"
9 strips, 2½" × 42"

## Making the Blocks

Press the seam allowances as indicated by the arrows, or as otherwise instructed.

**For each block, you'll use:**
3 different pairs of dark or medium 5" squares
1 dark or medium 5" square
2 different pairs of light 5" squares
1 light 5" square

1  Select one pair of dark or medium 5" squares and one pair of light 5" squares. Draw a diagonal line from corner to corner on the wrong side of the light squares. Place each marked square on a dark square, right sides together and raw edges aligned. Stitch ¼" from the lines on both sides and cut the squares apart on the drawn lines. Trim the four resulting half-square-triangle units to 4½" square, including seam allowances.

Make 4.

2  Cut one pair of dark or medium 5" squares into 2½" squares and one pair of light 5" squares into 2½" × 4½" rectangles. Draw a diagonal line on the wrong side of each dark or medium 2½" square. Place a marked square on one end of a light rectangle. Sew on the drawn line. Trim the excess fabric, leaving ¼" seam allowances, and press the seam allowances toward the resulting triangle. Repeat on the other end of the rectangle to complete a flying-geese unit. Use the marked squares and the rectangles to make four flying-geese units.

Make 4.

3 Trim ½" from one edge of one pair of dark or medium 5" squares. Cut the trimmed pieces in half in the opposite direction of the first cut to yield four rectangles, 2½" × 4½".

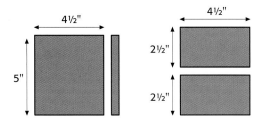

4 Sew a rectangle from step 3 to each flying-geese unit from step 2 as shown.

5 Trim a dark or medium 5" square to 4½" × 4½". Cut a light 5" square in half vertically and horizontally to yield four 2½" squares. Draw a diagonal line on the wrong side of the 2½" squares.

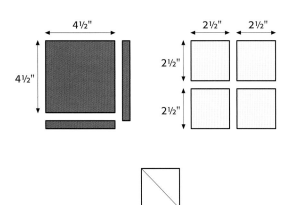

6 Position marked light squares on diagonally opposite corners of the medium 4½" square, right sides together. Sew along each drawn line. Trim the excess fabric, leaving ¼" seam allowances, and press. Repeat, sewing light squares to the remaining two corners of the medium square.

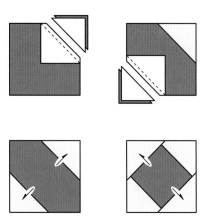

7 Arrange the four half-square-triangle units from step 1, the four flying-geese units from step 4, and the unit from step 6 into three rows as shown. Sew the units in each row together, and then join the rows.

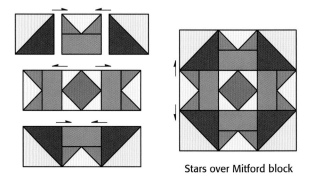

Stars over Mitford block

8 Repeat steps 1–7 to make a total of 35 blocks, using the diagrams below for alternate placement of the dark and medium fabrics if desired.

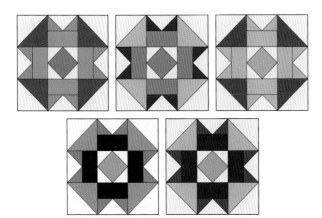

## Assembling the Quilt Top

1 Arrange the blocks in seven rows of five blocks each as shown in the quilt plan at right.

2 Sew the blocks together into rows and press the seam allowances in opposite directions from row to row. Sew the rows together, pressing the seam allowances in one direction.

3 Sew the medium 1½"-wide strips together end to end. Measure the length of the quilt top through the center and cut two strips to this measurement. Sew the strips to the sides of the quilt top and press the seam allowances toward the border. Measure the width of the quilt top through the center, including the borders just added. Cut two strips to this measurement and sew them to the top and bottom of the quilt top to complete the inner border. Press the seam allowances toward the border.

4 Repeat to add the dark 4¾"-wide strips for the outer border.

Quilt plan

## Finishing the Quilt

Refer to "Finishing Techniques" on page 236 for details on the following steps.

1 Layer and baste your quilt, and quilt as desired.

2 Using the dark 2½"-wide strips, prepare and attach the binding.

# Crossroads

**FINISHED QUILT:** 30½" × 30½" • **FINISHED BLOCK:** 11½" × 11½"

*Designed and made by Mary Etherington and Connie Tesene*

*This dandy little wall hanging or table topper is stitched in shades of gray, blue, and red to honor not only our country's independence, but also the fact that the United States emerged from the Civil War united, even after the nation's greatest period of strife.*

## Materials

*Yardage is based on 42"-wide fabric. Fat quarters are 18" × 21".*

13 assorted dark blue, gray, and red prints, 1 fat quarter each, for blocks, cornerstones, and pieced outer border

6 assorted light and medium-light prints, 1 fat quarter each, for blocks and pieced outer border

⅓ yard of red stripe for inner border

⅓ yard of dark blue print for binding

1 yard of fabric for backing

34" × 34" piece of batting

## Cutting

*All measurements include ¼"-wide seam allowances.*

### NINE-PATCH UNITS
*Cutting is for 1 unit. You'll need 16 total.*

**From 1 of the dark prints, cut:**
4 squares, 1¾" × 1¾"

**From 1 of the light or medium-light prints, cut:**
5 squares, 1¾" × 1¾"

### CENTER CROSS UNITS
*Cutting is for 1 unit. You'll need 4 total.*

**From 1 of the light or medium-light prints, cut:**
1 square, 3⅝" × 3⅝"; cut the square into quarters diagonally to yield 4 triangles

**From 1 of the dark prints, cut:**
4 rectangles, 1¾" × 3"

**From 1 of the dark prints, cut:**
1 square, 1¾" × 1¾"

### RAIL FENCE UNITS
**From the assorted dark, light, and medium-light prints, cut a *total* of:**
48 rectangles, 1¾" × 4½"

### BORDERS AND BINDING
**From the red stripe, cut:**
4 strips, 2" × 23½"

**From the dark prints, cut:**
4 squares, 2" × 2"
26 squares, 2⅞" × 2⅞"; cut the squares in half diagonally to yield 52 triangles
4 matching squares, 2½" × 2½"

**From the light and medium-light prints, cut:**
26 squares, 2⅞" × 2⅞"; cut the squares in half diagonally to yield 52 triangles

**From the dark blue print, cut:**
4 strips, 2¼" × 42"

## Making the Nine-Patch Units

Press the seam allowances as indicated by the arrows, or as otherwise instructed.

Lay out five light 1¾" squares and four matching dark 1¾" squares in three rows as shown. Sew the squares together into rows, and then join the rows. The unit should measure 4¼" square, including seam allowances. Make 16.

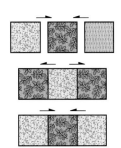 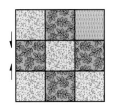

Make 16.

## Making the Center Cross Units

1 Using four matching light (or medium-light) 3⅝" triangles and four matching dark 1¾" × 3" rectangles, sew the light triangles, dark rectangles, and a dark 1¾" square together to make a center cross unit.

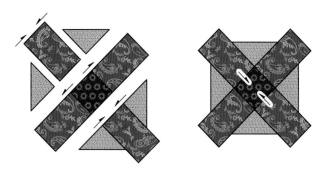

2 Trim the unit to measure 4½" square, including the seam allowances. Make four.

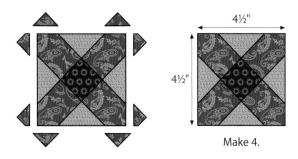

Make 4.

## Making the Rail Fence Units

Randomly sew three dark, light, and/or medium-light 1¾" × 4½" rectangles together along their long edges. The block should measure 4½" × 4¼", including seam allowances. Make 16.

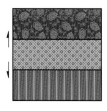

Make 16.

## Making the Crossroads Blocks

Randomly select four nine-patch units, four rail fence units, and one center cross unit, and lay them out in a nine-patch arrangement as shown. Sew the units together into rows, and then join the rows to complete a Crossroads block. The block should measure 12" square, including seam allowances. Make four blocks.

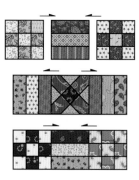
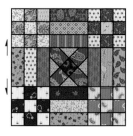

Make 4.

## Assembling the Quilt Top

1 Arrange the Crossroads blocks in two rows of two blocks each.

2 Sew the blocks together into rows, pressing the seam allowances in opposite directions from row to row. Join the rows and press the seam allowances in one direction.

3 Sew red-stripe 2"-wide strips to the top and bottom of the quilt top. Sew a dark 2" square to each end of the two remaining striped strips. Sew these strips to the sides of the quilt top.

4 Sew a pair of light and dark 2⅞" triangles together along the long edges. Press the seam allowances toward the dark triangle. Make 52 half-square-triangle units.

5 Sew 13 half-square-triangle units together, orienting the dark triangles in the same direction. Make four pieced borders.

Make 4.

6 Sew pieced border strips to the top and bottom of the quilt top, positioning the light edge of each strip toward the inner border. Sew a dark 2½" square to each end of the two remaining pieced strips. Sew these strips to the sides of the quilt top.

## Finishing the Quilt

Refer to "Finishing Techniques" on page 236 for details on the following steps.

1 Layer and baste your quilt, and quilt as desired.

2 Using the dark blue 2¼"-wide strips, prepare and attach the binding.

Quilt assembly

# Guest Room Quilt

**FINISHED QUILT:** 72½" × 72½" • **FINISHED BLOCKS:** 4" × 4" and 2" × 2"

*Designed and pieced by Biz Storms; quilted by Emma Hostetler*

*Influenced by a distinctive style of antique quilt, Biz Storms began with a densely pieced center area that she surrounded with hundreds of larger blocks. A single block design in two different sizes does all the work in this inviting creation.*

## Materials

*Yardage is based on 42"-wide fabric.*

4 yards *total* of assorted light prints for small and large blocks

⅜ yard *total* of assorted medium and dark blue prints for small blocks

Scrap of dark rust print for small blocks

3⅝ yards *total* of assorted medium and dark prints for large blocks

⅔ yard of fabric for binding

4½ yards of fabric for backing

80" × 80" piece of batting

## Cutting

*All measurements include ¼"-wide seam allowances.*

**From the assorted light prints, cut a *total* of:**

32 squares, 3¼" × 3¼"; cut the squares into quarters diagonally to yield 128 triangles

154 squares, 5¼" × 5¼"; cut the squares into quarters diagonally to yield 616 triangles

**From the assorted medium and dark blue prints, cut a *total* of:**

32 squares, 3¼" × 3¼"; cut the squares into quarters diagonally to yield 128 triangles (2 are extra)

**From the dark rust print, cut:**

1 square, 3¼" × 3¼"; cut the square into quarters diagonally to yield 4 triangles (2 are extra)

**From the assorted medium and dark prints, cut a *total* of:**

154 squares, 5¼" × 5¼"; cut the squares into quarters diagonally to yield 616 triangles

**From the binding fabric, cut:**

8 strips, 2¾" × 42"

## Making the Blocks

This quilt divides naturally into five sections for the designer's "batch-work method." Chain piecing makes the piecing proceed easily and efficiently. Once the blocks are made, you can work on assembling one section at a time. Check the direction of the seams in the adjacent blocks before pressing the rows in the adjoining sections. Press the seam allowances as indicated by the arrows, or as otherwise instructed.

1 Sort the small quarter-square triangles into matching pairs.

2 Divide the triangle pairs from step 1 into two stacks, one containing small light triangles and one containing small medium or dark blue and rust triangles. Work randomly so that identical pairs are not grouped together in either stack.

3 With right sides together, sew the top triangles from each stack together along one short side as shown on page 78. Without cutting the thread, sew the next light and medium or dark triangles

together. (These should match the first two triangles.) Continue chain piecing until you have reached the end of both stacks; cut the chain loose after sewing the last pair. You should have 128 triangle units in matching pairs.

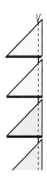

4 Cut the threads between each unit; press the seam allowances toward the darker triangles and carefully sort the units into two identical stacks as you go. Each stack should contain one of the matching triangle pairs.

5 With right sides together, long edges aligned, and opposing seam allowances carefully butted, sew the top unit from each stack together. Continue chain piecing until you have reached the end of both stacks. Cut the chain loose after sewing the last pair. Cut the threads between each unit and press. You now have 64 small blocks.

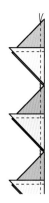 

Make 64.

6 Repeat steps 1–5 using the large light quarter-square triangles and the large medium and dark quarter-square triangles. Make 308 large blocks.

Make 308.

## Assembling the Quilt Top

1 Referring to section 1 of the assembly diagram at right, arrange the small blocks in eight rows of eight blocks each, rotating the blocks as shown, and placing the light/rust block near the center. Sew the blocks into rows. Press the seam allowances in opposite directions from row to row. Sew the rows together, carefully butting the seam allowances; press. Label this section 1.

2 Referring to sections 2 and 3 of the assembly diagram, arrange 28 large blocks in four horizontal rows of seven blocks each, rotating the blocks as shown. Sew the blocks into rows. Press the seam allowances in opposite directions from row to row. Sew the rows together; press. Make two and label them section 2 and section 3.

3 Referring to sections 4 and 5 of the assembly diagram, arrange 126 large blocks in seven horizontal rows of 18 blocks each, rotating the blocks as shown. Sew the blocks into rows. Press the seam allowances in opposite directions from row to row. Sew the rows together; press. Make two and label them section 4 and section 5.

4 Arrange the five sections of the quilt as shown. Sew sections 1, 2, and 3 together; press. Sew section 4 to the top and section 5 to the bottom; press the seam allowances away from the center.

## Finishing the Quilt

Refer to "Finishing Techniques" on page 236 for details on the following steps.

1 Layer and baste your quilt, and quilt as desired.

2 Using the 2¾"-wide binding strips, prepare and attach the binding.

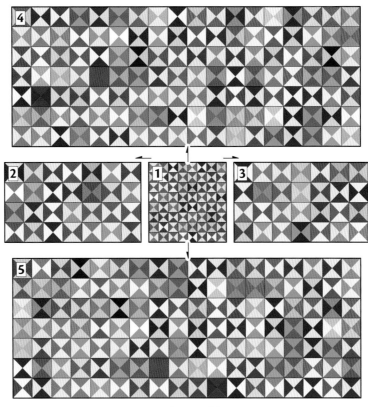

Quilt assembly

# Mary Smith's Dishrag

**FINISHED QUILT:** 23½" × 27½" • **FINISHED BLOCK:** 4" × 4"

*Designed and made by Carol Hopkins*

*Stories abound of women who secretly served in the Civil War to be with the men they loved, but the disguise was not always successful. Mary Smith's cover was reportedly blown by the way she wrung out a dishrag more thoroughly than a typical male soldier.*

## Materials

*Yardage is based on 42"-wide fabric.*

20 scraps, at least 8" × 8" each, of assorted medium or dark prints for blocks

20 scraps, at least 7" × 7" each, of assorted light prints for blocks

⅜ yard of black print for inner border and binding

½ yard of brown paisley for outer border

1⅛ yards of fabric for backing

29" × 33" piece of batting

## Cutting

*All measurements include ¼"-wide seam allowances.*

**From *each* of the 20 assorted medium or dark prints, cut:**

1 square, 4⅞" × 4⅞"; cut the square in half diagonally to yield 2 triangles (40 total; 20 are extra)

2 squares, 1⅞" × 1⅞"; cut the squares in half diagonally to yield 4 triangles (80 total)

1 square, 1½" × 1½" (20 total)

**From *each* of the 20 assorted light prints, cut:**

1 square, 2⅞" × 2⅞"; cut the square in half diagonally to yield 2 triangles (40 total; 20 are extra)

3 squares, 1⅞" × 1⅞"; cut the squares in half diagonally to yield 6 triangles (120 total)

**From the black print, cut:**

3 strips, 1" × 42"

3 strips, 2" × 42"

**From the brown paisley, cut:**

4 strips, 3½" × 42"

## Making the Blocks

Pair a different light and medium or dark print for each of the 20 blocks. Instructions are for making one block. Press the seam allowances as indicated by the arrows, or as otherwise instructed.

1 Sew together four matching medium or dark 1⅞" triangles and four matching light 1⅞" triangles to make four half-square-triangle units. Each unit should measure 1½" square, including seam allowances.

Make 4.

2 Sew together one light 1⅞" triangle and two half-square-triangle units. Then sew the unit to a matching light 2⅞" triangle.

3 Sew together one light 1⅞" light triangle, two half-square-triangle units, and one medium or dark square. Then sew this strip to the top of the unit from step 2.

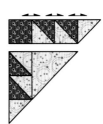 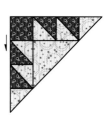

4 Sew the unit from step 3 to a matching medium or dark 4⅞" triangle. Repeat to make a total of 20 blocks that measure 4½" square, including seam allowances.

Make 20.

## Assembling the Quilt Top

1 Arrange the blocks into five rows of four blocks each as shown.

2 Sew the blocks together into rows, and then join the rows.

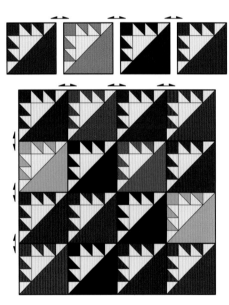

Quilt assembly

3 Measure the length of the quilt top through the center and trim two black 1"-wide strips to this measurement. Sew the strips to the sides of the quilt top. Measure the width of the quilt top through the center, including the borders just added. From the remaining black 1"-wide strip, trim two strips to this measurement. Sew the strips to the top and bottom of the quilt top.

4 Measure the length of the quilt top through the center and trim two paisley 3½"-wide strips to this measurement. Sew the strips to the sides of the quilt top. Measure the width of the quilt top through the center, including the borders just added, and trim the remaining paisley strips to this measurement. Sew the strips to the top and bottom of the quilt top.

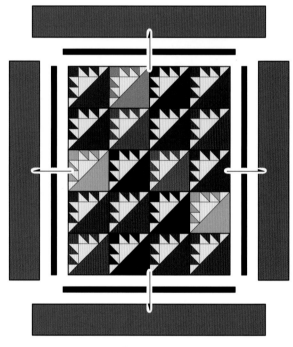

Adding borders

## Finishing the Quilt

Refer to "Finishing Techniques" on page 236 for details on the following steps.

1 Layer and baste your quilt, and quilt as desired.

2 Using the black 2"-wide strips, prepare and attach the binding.

# One Flag

**FINISHED QUILT:** 36½" × 36½" • **FINISHED BLOCKS:** 3" × 3", 2¼" × 2¼", and 2¼" × 4½"

*Designed and made by Mary Etherington and Connie Tesene*

*Don't let any bit of your reproduction fabrics—or your spare time—go to waste. This wall hanging lets you put all your leftovers to good use while incorporating the full palette of Civil War–era colors.*

## Materials

*Yardage is based on 42"-wide fabric. Fat quarters are 18" × 21".*

15 medium or dark prints, 1 fat quarter each, in black, navy, blue, teal, light blue, green, sour green, brown, red, pink, orange, gold, and rust for blocks and spacer squares

15 light or medium-light prints, 1 fat quarter each, for blocks

⅓ yard of dark brown print for binding

1¼ yards of fabric for backing

40" × 40" piece of batting

## Cutting

*All measurements include ¼"-wide seam allowances.*

### STAR BLOCKS
*Cutting is for 1 block. You'll need 45 total.*

**From *1* of the medium or dark prints, cut:**
1 square, 2" × 2"
8 squares, 1¼" × 1¼"

**From *1* of the light or medium-light prints, cut:**
4 rectangles, 1¼" × 2"
4 squares, 1¼" × 1¼"

### SPACER SQUARES
**From the assorted dark prints, cut:**
36 squares, 3½" × 3½"

### NINE PATCH BLOCKS
*Cutting is for 1 block. You'll need 53 total.*

**From *1* of the dark prints, cut:**
5 squares, 1¼" × 1¼"

**From *1* of the light prints, cut:**
4 squares, 1¼" × 1¼"

### REVERSE NINE PATCH BLOCKS
*Cutting is for 1 block. You'll need 53 total.*

**From *1* of the light prints, cut:**
5 squares, 1¼" × 1¼"

**From *1* of the dark prints, cut:**
4 squares, 1¼" × 1¼"

### FLAG BLOCK
**From *1* of the blue prints, cut:**
1 rectangle, 1¾" × 2¾"

**From *1* of the red prints, cut:**
3 rectangles, ¾" × 2¾"
2 rectangles, ¾" × 5"

**From *1* of the light prints, cut:**
2 rectangles, ¾" × 2¾"
2 rectangles, ¾" × 5"

### NINE PATCH ROWS
**From *1* of the red prints, cut:**
4 squares, 2¾" × 2¾"

### BINDING
**From the dark brown print, cut:**
4 strips, 2¼" × 42"

## Making the Star Blocks

Use one light (or medium-light) and one dark (or medium) print for each block. Press the seam allowances as indicated by the arrows, or as otherwise instructed.

1 Draw a diagonal line from corner to corner on the wrong side of each dark 1¼" square. Place a marked square on one end of a light rectangle, right sides together and corners aligned. Sew on

the drawn line. Trim the excess fabric of the dark square only, ¼" from the stitched line, and press. Repeat on the other end of the rectangle. Make four units.

Make 4.

2 Lay out the units from step 1, four light 1¼" squares, and one dark 2" square in rows. Sew the pieces together into rows, and then join the rows. The block should measure 3½" square, including seam allowances. Make 45 blocks.

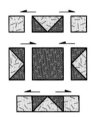 

Make 45.

## Making the Nine-Patch Star Blocks

Randomly select five Star blocks and four dark 3½" spacer squares and lay them out in a nine-patch arrangement, starting with a Star block in the top-left corner and alternating the blocks with the dark squares. Sew the blocks and plain squares together into rows, and then join the rows to complete a Nine-Patch Star block. The block should measure 9½" square, including seam allowances. Make nine blocks.

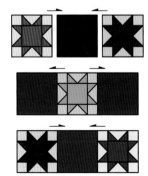 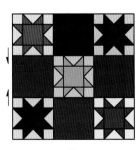

Make 9.

## Making the Nine Patch Blocks

1 Sew five matching dark 1¼" squares and four matching light 1¼" squares together into rows. Sew the rows together to make a Nine Patch block. Make 53 blocks.

Make 53.

2 Sew five matching light 1¼" squares and four matching dark 1¼" squares together into rows. Sew the rows together to make a reverse Nine Patch block. Make 53 blocks.

Make 53.

## Making the Nine Patch Sashing

Randomly select two Nine Patch blocks and two reverse Nine Patch blocks. Sew the blocks together, alternating them as shown to make a sashing strip. The sashing strip should measure 2¾" × 9½", including seam allowances. Make 12 strips.

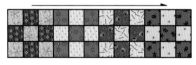

Make 12.

## Making the Flag Block

1. Sew the three red and two light ¾" × 2¾" rectangles together along their long edges.

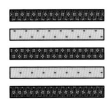 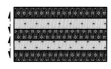

2. Sew the two red and two light ¾" × 5" rectangles together along their long edges.

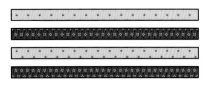

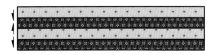

3. Sew the blue 1¾" × 2¾" rectangle to the left side of the unit from step 1. Sew this unit to the top edge of the unit from step 2 to complete the Flag block.

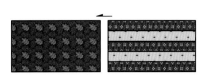

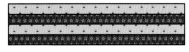

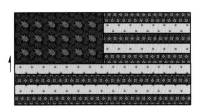

Make 1.

## Assembling the Quilt Top

1. Arrange the blocks, sashing strips, and red 2¾" squares as shown in the quilt assembly diagram at right.

2. Sew the pieces together into rows, and then join the rows.

3. Randomly select seven Nine Patch blocks and seven reverse Nine Patch blocks and sew them together, starting with a reverse Nine Patch block and alternating the blocks to make a side border. Repeat to make a second side border. Sew the Flag block, seven Nine Patch blocks, and seven reverse Nine Patch blocks together to make the top border of the quilt. Sew eight Nine Patch blocks and eight reverse Nine Patch blocks together to make the bottom border.

Side borders
Make 2.

Top border

Bottom border

4 Sew the side border strips to the quilt top first, and then add the top and bottom border strips.

## Finishing the Quilt

Refer to "Finishing Techniques" on page 236 for details on the following steps.

1 Layer and baste your quilt, and quilt as desired.

2 Using the dark brown 2¼"-wide strips, prepare and attach the binding.

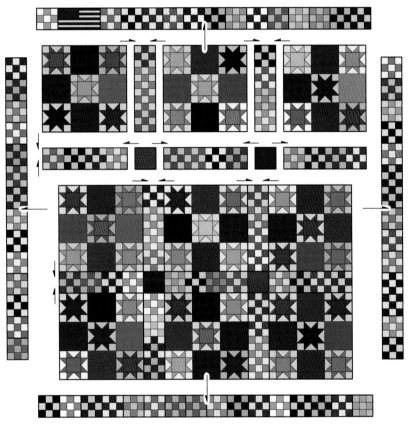

Quilt assembly

# Snow Day

**FINISHED QUILT:** 62¾" × 62¾" • **FINISHED BLOCK:** 9½" × 9½"

*Designed and made by Gayle Bong*

*This block is even more fun to make than the ever-popular Nine Patch, but just as easy. Perfect for a collection of 1800s reproduction fabrics, the design could also take a dramatic turn through the use of bold, contemporary colors and prints.*

## Materials

*Yardage is based on 42"-wide fabric.*

1⅜ yards *total* of assorted medium scraps for blocks

1¾ yards *total* of assorted dark scraps for blocks

8 assorted dark prints, ¼ yard each, for blocks, setting triangles, and cornerstones

1⅜ yards of muslin for blocks and sashing

⅝ yard of fabric for binding

3¾ yards of fabric for backing

68" × 68" piece of batting

## Cutting

*All measurements include ¼"-wide seam allowances.*

**From the assorted medium scraps, cut:**

24 strips, 3½" × 18"

**From the assorted dark scraps, cut:**

16 strips, 3½" × 25"; crosscut *each* strip into
4 rectangles, 3½" × 6" (64 total)

**From the 8 assorted dark prints, cut a *total* of:**

8 strips, 8¼" × 42"; crosscut:
- 4 rectangles, 3½" × 6", from *each* strip (32 total)
- 37 squares, 1¾" × 1¾"

Reserve the remainder of the dark prints for setting triangles.

**From the muslin, cut:**

3 strips, 3½" × 42"; crosscut into 24 squares, 3½" × 3½"

17 strips, 1¾" × 42"; crosscut into:
- 4 rectangles, 1¾" × 12"
- 60 rectangles, 1¾" × 10"

**From the binding fabric, cut:**

7 strips, 2¼" × 42"

## Making the Blocks

Press the seam allowances as indicated by the arrows, or as otherwise instructed.

1 Aligning the 45° line of a ruler with the upper long edge of a medium 3½" × 18" strip, trim the end of the strip near the lower-left corner as shown below. Discard the piece you've cut or add it to your scrap stash. Rotate the ruler so it is perpendicular to the first cut, align the 45° line with the bottom edge of the strip, and align the cutting edge of the ruler with the top edge of the strip to form a triangle. Cut. Repeat the process, alternating the ruler position, to cut 4 triangles from each medium strip, for a total of 96. Repeat to cut 2 triangles from the remainder of each dark print strip, for a total of 16. Set these dark triangles aside for quilt-top assembly.

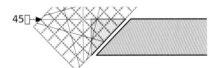

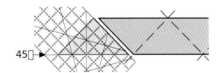

Cut 4 from each medium strip and 2 from each dark strip.

2 For each block, sew together a muslin 3½" square, four matching medium triangles from step 1, and four matching dark 3½" × 6" rectangles as shown. Make 24 blocks.

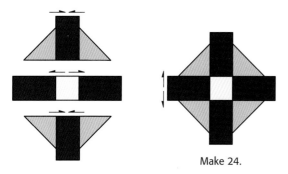

Make 24.

> **PLAN YOUR PAIRINGS**
> Before you start sewing the blocks, take some time to decide which medium print triangles and dark print rectangles go best together. (Now's the time to use that design wall!) If you have all of your fabrics paired up before you begin sewing, it's easy to chain piece the diagonal rows of the blocks quickly and efficiently.

3 Trim the blocks to 10" square, including seam allowances, by measuring 5" from the center point to trim each edge. If possible, use a large square ruler so you can measure and cut two edges without moving the ruler.

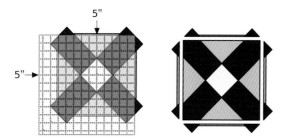

## Assembling the Quilt Top

1 Using the dark triangles that you set aside previously, sew a short edge of two different dark triangles to the sides of one muslin 1¾" × 12" strip as shown. The sashing strip will be longer than the triangles. Trim the excess sashing at the corner, using the edges of the triangles as a guide. Repeat to make a second corner unit.

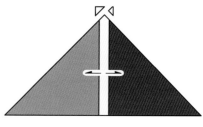

Make 2.

2 Arrange the blocks, muslin 1¾" × 10" sashing strips, dark 1¾" squares, side setting triangles, and corner units into rows as shown in the diagram below. Place the two remaining muslin 1¾" × 12" strips at the ends of the center sashing row.

3 Sew the pieces in each row together, and then join the rows. Add the two corner units last.

4 Square up the corners of the muslin 1¾" × 12" strips as in step 1.

5 Sew a line of stay stitching ³⁄₁₆" from the edges of the quilt top to prevent the seams from coming loose.

## Finishing the Quilt

Refer to "Finishing Techniques" on page 236 for details on the following steps.

1 Layer and baste your quilt, and quilt as desired.

2 Using the 2¼"-wide binding strips, prepare and attach the binding.

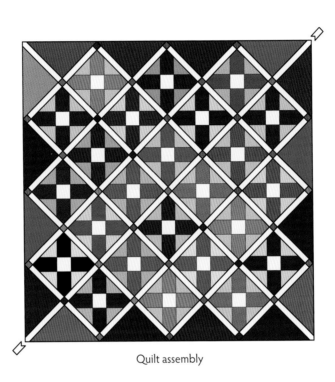

Quilt assembly

# Parlor Music

**FINISHED QUILT:** 37½" × 45½" • **FINISHED BLOCK:** 2" × 2"

*Designed and pieced by Carol Hopkins; quilted by Lisa Ramsey*

*During the Civil War, gathering to play and listen to music served as a venue for people to share, and endure, the events that dramatically impacted their lives. A range of multicolored light and dark prints harmonize beautifully in this well-orchestrated quilt.*

## Materials

*Yardage is based on 42"-wide fabric.*

20 scraps, at least 6" × 6" each, OR ⅞ yard *total* of assorted light prints for triangles

18 scraps, at least 6" × 6" each, OR ⅝ yard *total* of assorted dark prints for triangles

67 scraps, at least 4" × 4" each, OR ½ yard *total* of assorted light prints for Four Patch blocks

67 scraps, at least 4" × 4" each, OR ½ yard *total* of assorted dark prints for Four Patch blocks

1¼ yards of turquoise print for border and binding

3 yards of fabric for backing

46" × 54" piece of batting

## Cutting

*All measurements include ¼"-wide seam allowances.*

**From *each* of the light 6" × 6" scraps, cut:**

1 square, 5½" × 5½"; cut the square into quarters diagonally to yield 4 triangles (80 total)

**From *each* of the dark 6" × 6" scraps, cut:**

1 square, 5½" × 5½"; cut the square into quarters diagonally to yield 4 triangles (72 total)

**From *each* of the light 4" × 4" scraps, cut:**

4 squares, 1½" × 1½" (268 total; 2 are extra. Fabrics may be repeated.)

**From *each* of the dark 4" × 4" scraps, cut:**

4 squares, 1½" × 1½" (268 total; 2 are extra. Fabrics may be repeated.)

**From the turquoise print, cut on the *lengthwise* grain:**

4 strips, 4" × 45"

4 strips, 2" × 45"

## Making the Four Patch Strips

Press the seam allowances as indicated by the arrows, or as otherwise instructed.

1. Arrange two matching light and two matching dark 1½" squares as shown. Sew the pieces together in rows, and then sew the rows together to make a Four Patch block measuring 2½" square, including seam allowances. Make 133 Four Patch blocks.

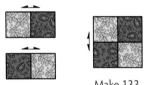

Make 133.

2. Sew 19 Four Patch blocks together to form a strip that measures 2½" × 38½", including seam allowances. Make seven strips.

Make 7.

## Making the Triangle Strips

1. Beginning with a light 5½" triangle, sew together 10 light triangles and nine dark triangles along the short sides of the triangles, alternating light and dark. The long sides of the triangles should be on the outside edges of the strip. Do not line up the triangles edge to edge; instead, offset the triangles by ¼" as shown.

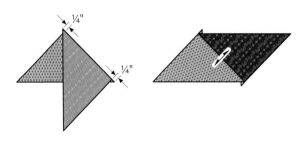

2 Press the seam allowances open after adding each triangle, being careful not to stretch the fabrics. The strip should end with a light triangle. Make eight strips.

Make 8.

## Assembling the Quilt Top

1 Beginning with a strip of triangles, arrange alternating strips of Four Patch blocks and triangles.

2 Cut the triangles at the top and bottom of the triangle strips in half crosswise so that they match the length of the Four Patch strips.

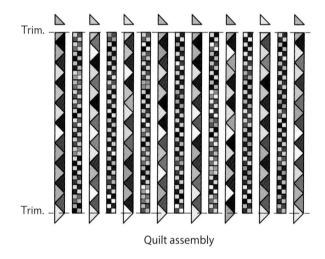

Quilt assembly

3 Sew all of the strips together, pressing the seam allowances open after adding each strip.

4 Measure the length of the quilt top through the center and trim two turquoise 4"-wide strips to this measurement. Sew the strips to the sides of the quilt top. Measure the width of the quilt top through the center, including the borders just added. Trim the remaining turquoise 4"-wide strips to this measurement and sew them to the top and bottom of the quilt top.

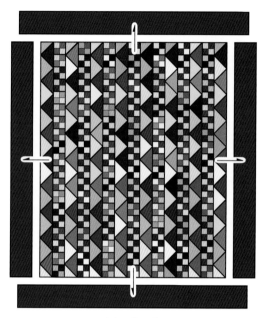

Adding borders

## Finishing the Quilt

Refer to "Finishing Techniques" on page 236 for details on the following steps.

1 Layer and baste your quilt, and quilt as desired.

2 Using the turquoise 2"-wide strips, prepare and attach the binding.

# Sweet and Sassy

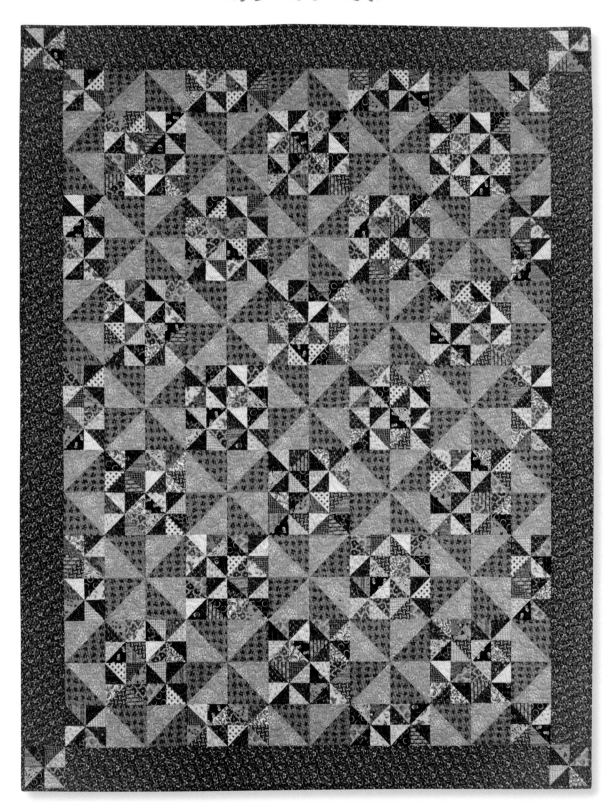

**FINISHED QUILT:** 56" × 72" • **FINISHED BLOCK:** 8" × 8"

*Designed by Evelyn Sloppy; made by Kathy Averett*

*Quiltmaker Kathy Averett loves pinks and browns, and she really has a flair for selecting just the right fabrics. Pinwheels twirl all over this quilt top, but thanks to simple half-square triangles, construction is much less complicated than it looks.*

## Materials

*Yardage is based on 42"-wide fabric.*

1 yard of pink print for large pinwheels

1 yard of light brown print for large pinwheels

1½ yards *total* of assorted dark pink and dark brown prints for small pinwheels

1½ yards *total* of assorted light pink and light brown prints for small pinwheels

1 yard of brown print for border

⅝ yard of fabric for binding

3⅝ yards of fabric for backing

60" × 76" piece of batting

## Cutting

*All measurements include ¼"-wide seam allowances.*

**From the pink print, cut:**
6 strips, 5" × 42"; crosscut into 48 squares, 5" × 5"

**From the light brown print, cut:**
6 strips, 5" × 42"; crosscut into 48 squares, 5" × 5"

**From the assorted dark pink and dark brown prints, cut a *total* of:**
200 squares, 3" × 3"

**From the assorted light pink and light brown prints, cut a *total* of:**
200 squares, 3" × 3"

**From the brown print for border, cut:**
6 strips, 4½" × 42"

**From the binding fabric, cut:**
7 strips, 2½" × 42"

## Making the Blocks

Press the seam allowances as indicated by the arrows, or as otherwise instructed.

1. Draw a diagonal line from corner to corner on the wrong side of the pink 5" squares. Place a marked square on a light brown 5" square, right sides together and raw edges aligned. Sew ¼" from the drawn line on both sides. Cut the squares apart on the line and press. Make 96 half-square-triangle units with the pink and light brown 5" squares. Trim the units to 4½" square, including seam allowances.

2. In the same manner, use the assorted pink and brown 3" squares to make 400 half-square-triangle units. Trim the units to 2½" square, including seam allowances. Sew four of these units together to make a pinwheel unit. Repeat to make 100 units that measure 4½" square, including seam allowances.

Make 100.

### PRESSING FOR SUCCESS
When making Pinwheel blocks, there can be a lot of bulk where the points all come together. Pressing the seam allowances open can help alleviate this bulk. Try it both ways to see which you prefer.

3 Sew together two half-square-triangle units from step 1 and two pinwheel units from step 2 to complete the block. Make 48 blocks. They should measure 8½" square, including seam allowances.

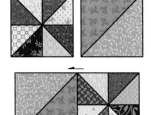
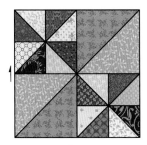

Make 48.

## Assembling the Quilt Top

1 Lay out the blocks in eight rows of six blocks each as shown, paying close attention to the orientation of each block.

2 Sew the blocks together into rows; press. Sew the rows together and press the seam allowances in one direction.

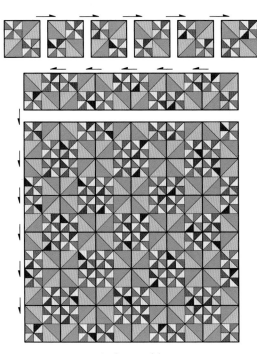

Quilt assembly

3 Sew the brown 4½"-wide strips together end to end. Measure the length and width of the quilt top through the center and cut two strips to each measurement. Sew the longer strips to the sides of the quilt top and press the seam allowances toward the borders. Sew the four remaining small pinwheel units to the ends of the shorter strips, pressing the seam allowances toward the strips. Sew these strips to the top and bottom of the quilt top and press the seam allowances toward the borders.

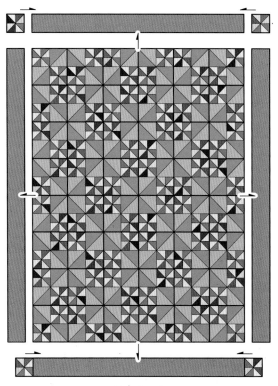

Adding borders

## Finishing the Quilt

Refer to "Finishing Techniques" on page 236 for details on the following steps.

1 Layer and baste your quilt, and quilt as desired.

2 Using the 2½"-wide binding strips, prepare and attach the binding.

# Market Baskets

**FINISHED QUILT:** 60½" × 60½" • **FINISHED BLOCK:** 12" × 12"

*Designed and made by Kim Brackett*

*Richly colored reproduction prints really capture the look of an antique quilt, but you could just as easily go cheerful and happy with bright colors. Either way, these baskets will make a very impressive dent in your fabric stash.*

## Materials

*Yardage is based on 42"-wide fabric.*

44 strips, 2½" × 42", of assorted dark prints for blocks
25 strips, 2½" × 42", of assorted light prints for blocks
⅝ yard of brown print for binding
4¼ yards of fabric for backing
64½" × 64½" piece of batting

## Cutting

*All measurements include ¼"-wide seam allowances.*

**From *each* of 25 assorted dark print strips, cut:**
6 rectangles, 2½" × 4½" (150 total)*
4 squares, 2½" × 2½" (100 total)

**From *each* of 19 assorted dark print strips, cut:**
8 rectangles, 2½" × 4½" (152 total)*

**From *each* of the 25 assorted light print strips, cut:**
2 rectangles, 2½" × 6½" (50 total)
8 squares, 2½" × 2½" (200 total)

**From the brown print, cut:**
7 strips, 2½" × 42"

*\*You will have a total of 302 dark print 2½" × 4½" rectangles; 2 are extra.*

### CUTTING FROM SCRAPS

For each block choose one basket fabric, one background fabric, and assorted scraps for the border. Cut the following number of pieces for each of the 25 blocks.

**From the basket fabric, cut:**
2 rectangles, 2½" × 4½" (50 total)
4 squares, 2½" × 2½" (100 total)

**From the background fabric, cut:**
2 rectangles, 2½" × 6½" (50 total)
8 squares, 2½" × 2½" (200 total)

**From the assorted block border fabrics, cut:**
10 rectangles, 2½" × 4½" (250 total)

*See "Cutting" at left for instructions on cutting the binding.*

## Making the Units

Press the seam allowances as indicated by the arrows, or as otherwise instructed.

1. Draw a diagonal line from corner to corner on the wrong side of a light 2½" square. Place the marked square on a dark 2½" square, right sides together and raw edges aligned. Sew on the drawn line. Trim ¼" from the line on one side and press. Make four half-square-triangle units for each block (100 total).

Make 4
for each block.

2. Sew a light 2½" square to a dark side of a half-square-triangle unit as shown. Make two for each block (50 total).

Make 2
for each block.

3 Sew together the two units from step 2. Carefully clip the seam allowances at the intersection of the units; clip up to, but *not through,* the stitching. Press the seam allowances in a clockwise direction. Make one unit for each block (25 total).

Make 1
for each block.

4 Draw a diagonal line from corner to corner on the wrong side of a light 2½" square. Place the marked square on one end of a dark 2½" × 4½" rectangle, right sides together and corners aligned. Sew on the drawn line. Trim the excess fabric, ¼" from the stitched line, and press the seam allowances toward the light triangle. Make one for each block (25 total).

Make 1
for each block.

5 Sew together the units from steps 3 and 4 as shown. Make one for each block (25 total).

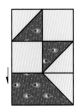

Make 1
for each block.

6 Referring to step 4, reverse the stitching angle to make a mirror-image unit using a light 2½" square and a dark 2½" × 4½" rectangle. Press the seam allowances toward the light triangle. Make one for each block (25 total).

Make 1
for each block.

7 Sew the unit from step 6 to a half-square-triangle unit from step 1 as shown. Make one for each block (25 total).

Make 1
for each block.

8 Sew together the units from steps 5 and 7 as shown. Make one for each block (25 total).

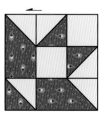

Make 1
for each block.

## Assembling the Blocks

1 Sew two 2½" × 6½" rectangles and the remaining half-square-triangle unit to the unit from step 8 as shown. Make 25 basket units.

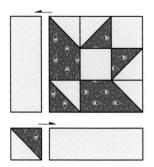 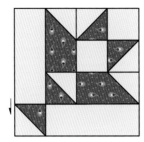

Make 25.

2 Using 10 assorted 2½" × 4½" rectangles, add the block border to each basket unit as shown. Make 25 blocks.

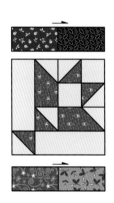 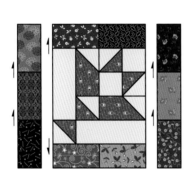

Make 25.

## Assembling the Quilt Top

1 Arrange the blocks in five rows of five blocks each as shown.

2 Sew the blocks together into rows; press. Sew the rows together and press the seam allowances in one direction.

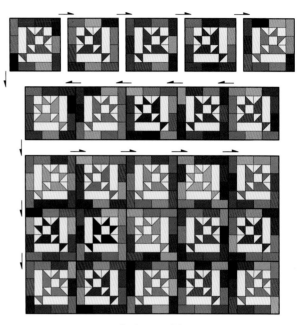

Quilt assembly

## Finishing the Quilt

Refer to "Finishing Techniques" on page 236 for details on the following steps.

1 Layer and baste your quilt, and quilt as desired.

2 Using the brown 2½"-wide strips, prepare and attach the binding.

# Sister's Choice

**FINISHED QUILT:** 64½" × 74½" • **FINISHED BLOCK:** 10" × 10"

*Designed and made by Julie Hendricksen*

*Give a variety of blue prints an extra dash of interest by mixing in black fabrics for the Sister's Choice blocks and Sawtooth border. When the blocks are set together with large half-square-triangle units, the design really comes alive.*

## Materials

*Yardage is based on 42"-wide fabric. Fat quarters are 18" × 21".*

11 fat quarters of assorted indigo prints for blocks and border

7 fat quarters of assorted black prints for blocks and border

2⅞ yards of muslin for blocks, setting squares, and border

1⅓ yards of blue print for setting squares

⅔ yard of indigo print for binding

4⅞ yards of fabric for backing

77" × 87" piece of batting

## Cutting

*All measurements include ¼"-wide seam allowances.*

**From *each* of the indigo fat quarters, cut:**

2 strips, 2½" × 21"; crosscut into 16 squares, 2½" × 2½" (176 total; 16 are extra)

2 strips, 2⅞" × 21"; crosscut into 11 squares, 2⅞" × 2⅞". Cut the squares in half diagonally to yield 22 triangles (242 total; 7 are extra).

**From *each* of the 7 black fat quarters, cut:**

3 strips, 2⅞" × 21"; crosscut into 18 squares, 2⅞" × 2⅞". Cut the squares in half diagonally to yield 36 triangles (252 total; 17 are extra).

**From the muslin, cut:**

4 strips, 10⅞" × 42"; crosscut into 11 squares, 10⅞" × 10⅞".* Cut the squares in half diagonally to yield 22 triangles (1 is extra).

12 strips, 2½" × 42"; crosscut into 189 squares, 2½" × 2½"

6 strips, 2⅞" × 42"; crosscut into 67 squares, 2⅞" × 2⅞". Cut the squares in half diagonally to yield 134 triangles.

**From the blue print, cut:**

4 strips, 10⅞" × 42"; crosscut into 11 squares, 10⅞" × 10⅞".* Cut the squares in half diagonally to yield 22 triangles (1 is extra).

**From the indigo print for binding, cut:**

8 strips, 2½" × 42"

*\*If you prefer, cut the muslin and blue squares to be 11" instead of 10⅞" for a bit of leeway when assembling the quilt top.*

## Making the Blocks

You have cut enough pieces to make 22 blocks, but only 21 are needed. Make the extra block and save it for another project if you wish. Each indigo print is used in two blocks, six black prints are used in three blocks, and one black print is used in four blocks. Press the seam allowances as indicated by the arrows, or as otherwise instructed.

1 Sew an indigo 2⅞" triangle to a black 2⅞" triangle along the diagonal to make a half-square-triangle unit. The unit should measure 2½" square, including seam allowances. Repeat to make a total of eight half-square-triangle units using the same indigo and black fabrics.

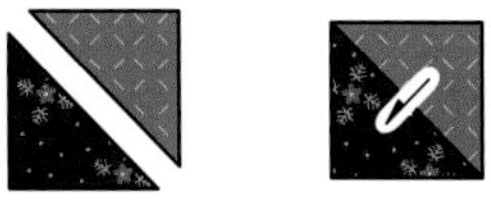

Make 8.

2 Sew together five muslin 2½" squares and four indigo 2½" squares (matching the indigo used in step 1) to make a Nine Patch block. The block should measure 5" square, including seam allowances.

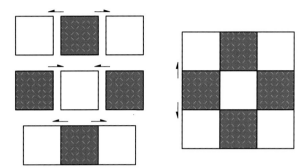

3 Lay out the half-square-triangle units from step 1, the Nine Patch block, four muslin 2½" squares, and four matching indigo 2½" squares as shown. Sew the pieces together into rows, and then join the rows. The block should measure 10½" square, including seam allowances. Repeat to make a total of 21 blocks.

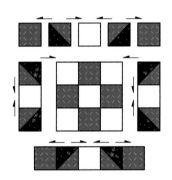
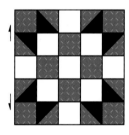

Make 21.

## Making the Setting Squares

Sew a blue 10⅞" triangle to a muslin 10⅞" triangle along the diagonal to make a half-square-triangle unit. The pieced unit should measure 10½" square, including seam allowances. Repeat to make a total of 21 units for setting squares.

Make 21.

## Making the Border Units

Sew an indigo 2⅞" triangle to a muslin 2⅞" triangle along the diagonal to make a half-square-triangle unit. Press the seam allowances toward the indigo print. The half-square-triangle unit should measure 2½" square, including seam allowances. Make a total of 67 units using the indigo prints and muslin. Repeat to make a total of 67 units using the black prints and muslin.

Make 67 indigo and 67 black.

## Assembling the Quilt Top

1 Lay out the blocks and setting squares in seven rows of six blocks and squares each as shown in the assembly diagram at right. (As a wink to the idiosyncrasies of antique quilts, designer Julie Hendricksen added her own twist by rotating the block in the lower-right corner one turn out of alignment.)

2 Sew the blocks and squares together into rows, and then join the rows. The quilt center should measure 60½" × 70½", including seam allowances.

3 Sew together 30 border units as shown for the top border, using a random combination of indigo and black prints. Press the seam allowances in one direction. Repeat to make a second border for the bottom of the quilt, noting that the triangles are angled in the opposite direction. Sew the border strips to the quilt top, positioning the white edges of the triangles toward the quilt center.

4 In the same manner, sew together 37 border units for the side border and press the seam allowances in one direction. Repeat to make a second border, again noting that the triangles are angled in the opposite direction. Sew the side borders to the quilt top with the white triangles toward the quilt center.

## Finishing the Quilt

Refer to "Finishing Techniques" on page 236 for details on the following steps.

1 Layer and baste your quilt, and quilt as desired.

2 Using the indigo 2½"-wide strips, prepare and attach the binding.

Quilt assembly

# Echoing Squares

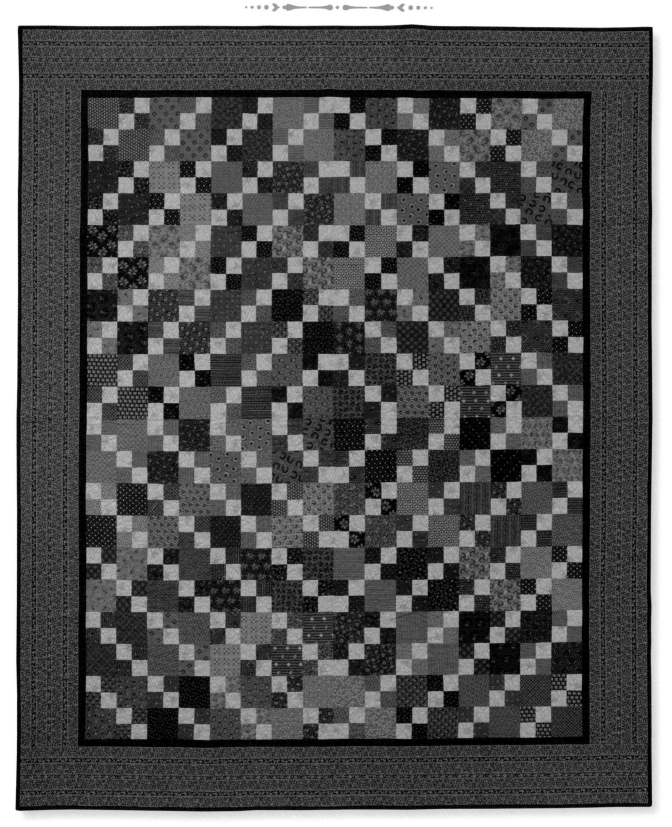

**FINISHED QUILT:** 82½" × 98½" • **FINISHED BLOCK:** 8" × 8"

*Designed and made by Lynn Roddy Brown*

*Reproduction prints mesh beautifully with other fabrics in similar shades to give this quilt its appealing old-fashioned flavor. A contrasting light print creates the distinct diagonal chain, and you can alter the border width based on the striped fabric you choose.*

## Materials

*Yardage is based on 42"-wide fabric.*

60 strips, 5½" × 20", of assorted medium and dark prints for blocks

2 yards of beige print for four-patch units

1⅜ yards of burgundy print for inner border and binding

2⅞ yards of brown stripe for outer border

8¼ yards of fabric for backing

91" × 107" piece of batting

## Cutting

*All measurements include ¼"-wide seam allowances.*

**From the beige print, cut:**

6 strips, 10½" × 42"; crosscut into 40 rectangles, 5½" × 10½"

**From the burgundy print, cut:**

9 strips, 1½" × 42"

10 strips, 2½" × 42"

**From the brown stripe, cut on the *lengthwise* grain:**

4 strips, 8½" × 94"*

*\*You may need to cut your border strips slightly wider or narrower, depending on the width of the stripe repeat in your fabric. Refer to "Fussy Cutting Stripes" above right.*

## FUSSY CUTTING STRIPES

To fussy cut a lengthwise stripe, first study the fabric to find one stripe or a combination of stripes that will approximately equal the desired width. When you've selected the stripe, you must add a ¼" seam allowance to each side. Lay the ¼" line of a rotary ruler on the line of the stripe you're using. Cut one layer at a time. Lynn Roddy Brown recommends using a short ruler and realigning often. Turn the fabric and add a ¼" seam to the other edge of the stripe.

When sewing the striped border strips to the quilt, place the striped fabric on top, with the right side down. On the wrong side of the fabric, you should be able to see the stripe. Use the line in the fabric as a sewing line. It's more important visually to follow the stripe so that it won't be wavy or cut off on the right side of the quilt.

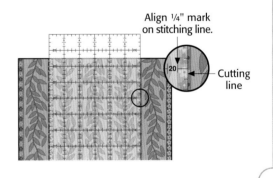

## Making the Blocks

Press the seam allowances as indicated by the arrows, or as otherwise instructed.

Blocks are made in sets of four. For each set of blocks, you'll need:

- 3 medium or dark strips, 5½" × 20"

- 2 beige rectangles, 5½" × 10½"

1 Cut two of the medium or dark strips into one 5½" × 10½" rectangle and two 4½" squares each as shown.

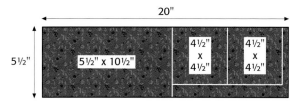

Fabric 1

Fabric 2

2 Cut the remaining medium or dark strip into four 4½" squares.

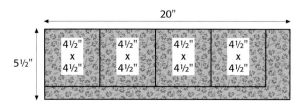

Fabric 3

3 Place a beige 5½" × 10½" rectangle on your ironing board, right side up, and spray evenly with spray starch. Layer a medium or dark 5½" × 10½" rectangle on top, right side down and edges aligned. Press well. Straighten the left edge with a ruler and rotary cutter, and then cut four 2½" × 5½" segments as shown. Repeat with a second pair of beige and medium or dark rectangles for a total of eight segments.

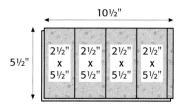

4 Sew each layered segment along one long edge, creating small strip sets. Press the seam allowances toward the darker fabric.

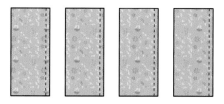

5 Pair the small strip sets, with right sides together and seam allowances opposing. Lay each unit on the cutting mat, trim the left edge, and then cut two 2½" segments. You may wish to place one pin in the cross seam to hold the pieces together as you remove them from your cutting mat.

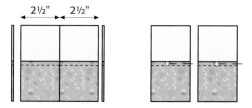

6 Sew each layered segment along one long edge to create a four-patch unit. Press the seam allowances open. Make a total of eight four-patch units.

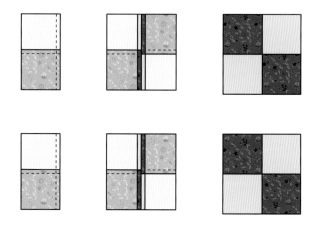

7 Arrange the four-patch units from step 6 and the 4½" squares from steps 1 and 2 into four blocks, varying the placement of the fabrics as shown and paying close attention to the orientation of the beige print in each four-patch unit.

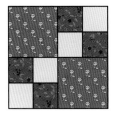

Fabrics 1 and 2

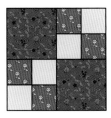

Fabrics 1 and 2

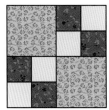

Fabrics 2 and 3

Fabrics 1 and 3

8 Sew the pieces together into rows and press. Sew the rows together and press the seam allowances open.

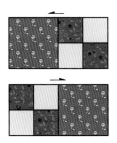

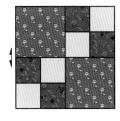

9 Repeat steps 1–8 to make a total of 80 blocks, keeping them organized in 20 sets of 4.

## Assembling the Quilt Top

1 Lay out the quilt top in quadrants, each containing five rows of four blocks each. Within each quadrant, use one block from each of the 20 sets. Turn the blocks to create the diagonal chains as shown.

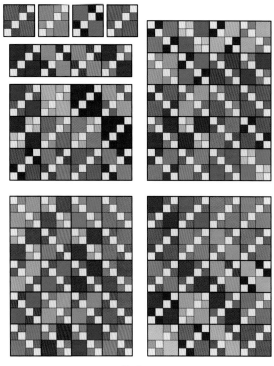

Quilt diagram

2 Sew the blocks of each quadrant into rows. Press the seam allowances open. Join the rows, and press the seam allowances open. Join the quadrants to complete the quilt top, and press.

3 For each of the side inner borders, sew two burgundy 1½"-wide strips together end to end, using a diagonal seam. Cut an additional burgundy strip into two equal lengths. Sew one of these half strips to each pieced strip. Press the

seam allowances open. Measure the length of the quilt top through the center and trim each long pieced strip to this measurement. Sew these strips to the sides of the quilt top and press the seam allowances toward the borders. For the top and bottom inner borders, sew two burgundy 1½"-wide strips together end to end, using a diagonal seam. Make two. Press the seam allowances open. Sew these strips to the top and bottom of the quilt top and press the seam allowances toward the borders.

4 Measure the length of the quilt top through the center. Trim two striped 8½" × 94" strips to this measurement and sew them to the sides of the quilt top. Press the seam allowances toward the inner border. Measure the width of the quilt top, including the borders just added. Trim the remaining striped strips to this measurement and sew them to the top and bottom edges of the quilt top. Press the seam allowances toward the inner border.

## Finishing the Quilt

Refer to "Finishing Techniques" on page 236 for details on the following steps.

1 Layer and baste your quilt, and quilt as desired.

2 Using the burgundy 2½"-wide strips, prepare and attach the binding.

# Calico Comfort Nine Patch

**FINISHED QUILT:** 63" × 73½" • **FINISHED BLOCK:** 7½" × 7½"

*Designed and made by Kathleen Tracy*

*Many women during the Civil War made quilts for family members going off to join the battle. Quilts made specifically for this purpose were mostly utilitarian and often consisted of scraps sewn into a simple pattern, such as Nine Patch blocks.*

## Materials

*Yardage is based on 42"-wide fabric.*

43 sets of 4 matching squares, 2" × 2", of medium and dark prints for blocks (172 total)

7 sets of 4 matching squares, 2" × 2", of light prints for blocks (28 total)

28 strips, 2" × 20", of assorted medium and dark prints for blocks

22 strips, 2" × 20", of assorted light prints for blocks

1 yard *total* of assorted medium and dark print scraps for block centers

¼ yard *total* of assorted light print scraps for block centers

1 yard of blue print for setting triangles

2 yards of black print for border

⅝ yard of brown print for binding

4½ yards of fabric for backing

71" × 81" piece of batting

## Cutting

*All measurements include ¼"-wide seam allowances.*

**From *each* of the 28 medium and dark print strips, cut:**

4 rectangles, 2" × 5" (112 total)

**From *each* of the 22 light print strips, cut:**

4 rectangles, 2" × 5" (88 total)

**From the assorted medium and dark print scraps for block centers, cut:**

40 squares, 5" × 5"

**From the assorted light print scraps for block centers, cut:**

10 squares, 5" × 5"

**From the blue print, cut:**

5 squares, 12" × 12"; cut the squares into quarters diagonally to yield 20 triangles (2 are extra)

2 squares, 6¼" × 6¼"; cut the squares in half diagonally to yield 4 triangles

**From the black print, cut on the *lengthwise* grain:**

4 strips, 5¼" × 72"

**From the brown print, cut:**

8 strips, 2½" × 42"

## Making the Blocks

Press the seam allowances as indicated by the arrows, or as otherwise instructed.

1 Lay out four matching 2" squares, four matching 2" × 5" rectangles, and one contrasting 5" square as shown.

2 Sew the pieces together into rows, and then join the rows. Make 50 blocks.

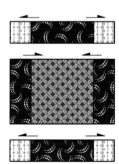 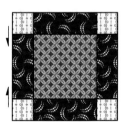

Make 50.

## Assembling the Quilt Top

1 Lay out the blocks and the blue side and corner triangles in diagonal rows as shown.

2 Sew the blocks and side triangles together into rows. Sew the rows together, matching seam intersections. Add the corner triangles and press the seam allowances toward the triangles.

Quilt assembly

3 Trim the quilt top, leaving a ¼" seam allowance beyond the points of the blocks.

4 Measure the length of the quilt top through the center. Trim two black 5¼"-wide strips to this measurement and sew them to the sides of the quilt top. Measure the width of the quilt top through the center, including the borders just added. Trim the remaining black strips to this measurement and sew them to the top and bottom of the quilt top.

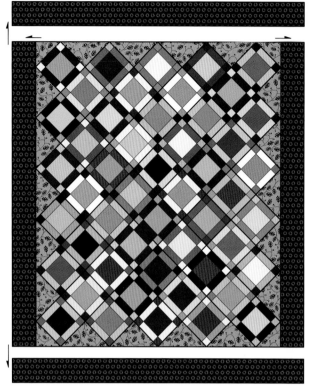

Adding borders

## Finishing the Quilt

Refer to "Finishing Techniques" on page 236 for details on the following steps.

1 Layer and baste your quilt, and quilt as desired.

2 Using the brown 2½"-wide strips, prepare and attach the binding.

# Alexander's Bean Pot

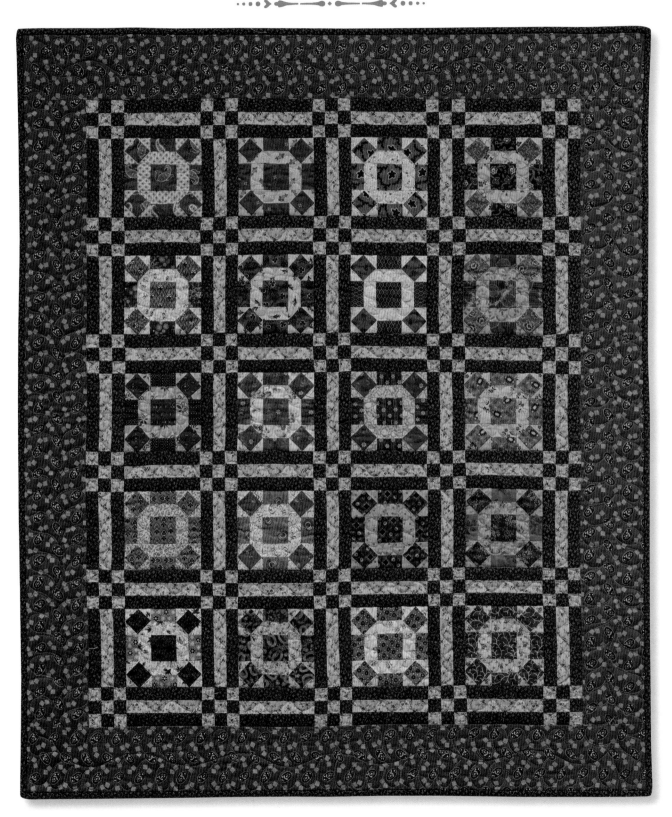

**FINISHED QUILT:** 36¾" × 43½" • **FINISHED BLOCK:** 4½" × 4½"

*Designed and made by Carol Hopkins*

*A century and a half later, the Civil War still stirs our emotions and imaginations. Carol Hopkins named this quilt for her brother-in-law, believing that had he been a soldier, his culinary flair with even a meager staple like dried beans would have earned him the job of cook.*

## Materials

*Yardage is based on 42"-wide fabric.*

20 scraps, at least 9" × 9" each, of assorted light prints for blocks

20 scraps, at least 9" × 9" each, of assorted dark prints for blocks

1 yard of red print for sashing and binding

½ yard of tan print for sashing

1⅛ yards of gold print for border

1⅝ yards of fabric for backing

42" × 49" piece of batting

## Cutting

*All measurements include ¼"-wide seam allowances. Different light and dark fabrics are used in each block; keep the fabrics for each block separate.*

### BLOCKS

*Cutting is for 1 block. You'll need 20 total.*

**From a light print, cut:**
1 strip, 1¼" × 8"
16 squares, 1¼" × 1¼"

**From a dark print, cut:**
1 strip, 1¼" × 8"
5 squares, 2" × 2"

### SASHING, BORDERS, AND BINDING

**From the red print, cut:**
18 strips, 1¼" × 42"
5 strips, 2" × 42"

**From the tan print, cut:**
12 strips, 1¼" × 42"

**From the gold print, cut on the *lengthwise* grain:**
4 strips, 4" × 39"

> **MIXING IT UP**
> Make a few three-color blocks by substituting a different dark fabric for the corner and center squares.

## Making the Blocks

Because this is a scrappy quilt, instructions are for making one block at a time. Press the seam allowances as indicated by the arrows, or as otherwise instructed.

1 To make the square-in-a-square units, place a light 1¼" square on one corner of a dark 2" square, right sides together. Sew diagonally across the light square as shown and press in place.

2 In the same manner, add a second light 1¼" square to an adjacent corner of the same dark square.

3 Repeat step 1 to add light squares to the remaining corners of the dark square. Make four square-in-a-square units.

Make 4.

4 Sew a light 1¼" × 8" strip and a dark 1¼" × 8" strip together along their long edges as shown to make a strip set. Crosscut the strip set into four segments, 2" wide.

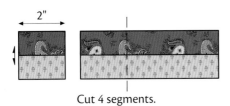

Cut 4 segments.

5 Lay out the four square-in-a-square units, the four strip-set segments, and a dark 2" square as shown. Sew the pieces together in rows, and then sew the rows together to complete the block. Repeat to make a total of 20 blocks that measure 5" square, including seam allowances.

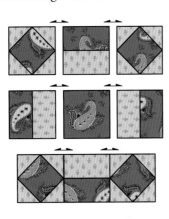

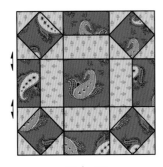

Make 20.

## Making the Sashing Units

1 Sew two red 1¼"-wide strips and one tan 1¼"-wide strip together along their long edges to make a strip set. Make eight strip sets. Crosscut the strip sets into 49 sashing strips, 5" wide, and 30 segments, 1¼" wide.

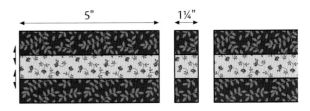

Make 8 strip sets.
Cut 49 sashing strips, 5" wide,
and 30 segments, 1¼" wide.

2 Sew two tan 1¼"-wide strips and one red 1¼"-wide strip together along their long edges to make a strip set. Make two strip sets. Crosscut the strip sets into 60 segments, 1¼" wide.

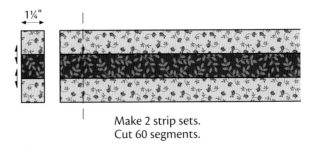

Make 2 strip sets.
Cut 60 segments.

3 Sew together two segments from step 2 and one 1¼"-wide segment from step 1 as shown. Make a total of 30 nine-patch units that measure 2¾" square, including seam allowances.

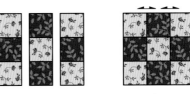

Make 30.

## Assembling the Quilt Top

1 Lay out the blocks in five rows of four blocks each, arranging them with the 5"-wide sashing strips and the nine-patch units as shown in the diagram below.

2 Sew the pieces together into rows, and then join the rows.

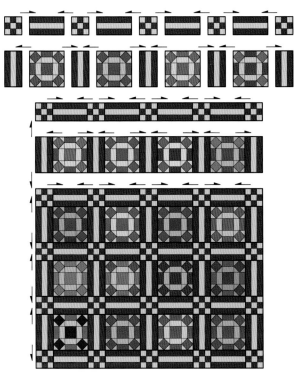

Quilt assembly

3 Measure the length of the quilt top through the center. Trim two gold 4"-wide strips to this measurement and sew them to the sides of the quilt top. Measure the width of the quilt top through the center, including the borders just added. Trim the remaining gold strips to this measurement and sew them to the top and bottom of the quilt top.

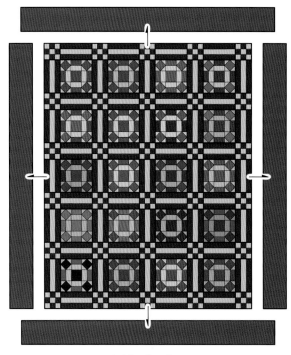

Adding borders

## Finishing the Quilt

Refer to "Finishing Techniques" on page 236 for details on the following steps.

1 Layer and baste your quilt, and quilt as desired.

2 Using the red 2"-wide strips, prepare and attach the binding.

# Wassenaar Windmills

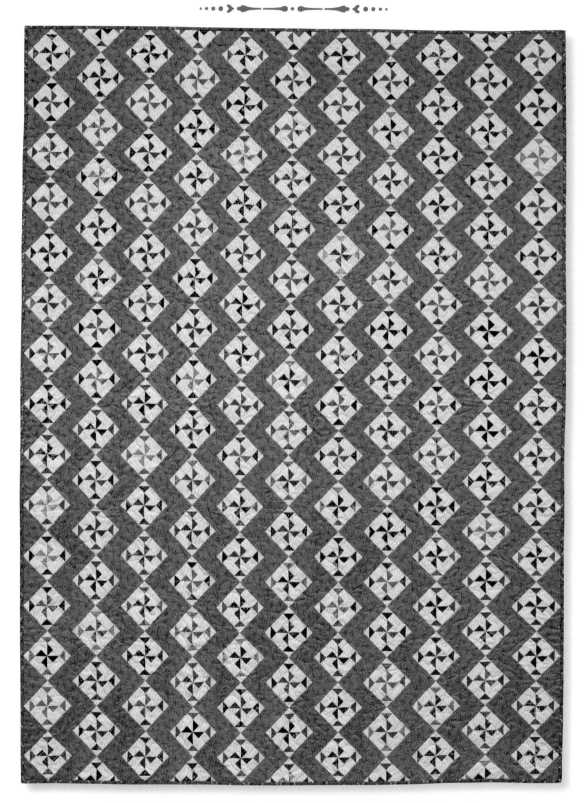

**FINISHED QUILT:** 63¾" × 85½" • **FINISHED BLOCK:** 4" × 4"

*Designed and pieced by Mary Elizabeth Kinch; quilted by Margaret Mitchell; machine-quilting design by Ellen Munnich*

*Whimsical windmill blocks are captivating as they spin across the quilt top in different combinations of lush browns and purples, warm caramels, and rich madder reds. The zigzag setting really adds to the joyous energy of the block.*

## Materials

*Yardage is based on 42"-wide fabric.*

2 yards *total* of assorted purple, brown, and madder-red prints for blocks

3¼ yards of muslin for blocks

3¾ yards of purple print for setting triangles

½ yard of fabric for binding

5⅝ yards of fabric for backing

70" × 92" piece of batting

## Cutting

*All measurements include ¼"-wide seam allowances.*

**From the assorted purple, brown, and madder-red prints, cut a *total* of:**

656 squares, 1⅞" × 1⅞", in matching pairs; cut the squares in half diagonally to yield 1312 triangles (2 are extra)

5 squares, 2¼" × 2¼"; cut the squares into quarters diagonally to yield 20 triangles

**From the muslin, cut:**

655 squares, 1⅞" × 1⅞"; cut the squares in half diagonally to yield 1310 triangles

5 squares, 2¼" × 2¼"; cut the squares into quarters diagonally to yield 20 triangles

660 rectangles, 1½" × 2½"

**From the purple print for setting triangles, cut:**

12 squares, 3¾" × 3¾"; cut the squares in half diagonally to yield 24 triangles

80 squares, 7" × 7"; cut the squares into quarters diagonally to yield 320 triangles (2 are extra)

**From the binding fabric, cut:**

8 strips, 1¾" × 42"

## Making the Blocks

Press the seam allowances as indicated by the arrows, or as otherwise instructed.

To avoid feeling overwhelmed by all the different fabrics in this quilt, organize the fabric into units, with each block using one set of matching fabrics for the pinwheel center and a different set of matching fabrics for the spinners on the outside. Break up the task of block assembly into "batch work," chain piecing five to eight blocks in one sitting. Sew a scrap of fabric (a thread pad) after the pieces for each block to act as a marker; that way you can keep track of sets that belong together in a block, allowing you to stop and restart easily as time permits.

1 Chain piece assorted print and muslin 1⅞" half-square triangles to make four matching half-square-triangle units. Finger-press the seam allowances toward the darker fabric. Continue in this manner to make 320 sets of 4 matching units (1,280 units total).

Make 4 matching units
(1280 total).

2 Sew four matching half-square-triangle units together to make a pinwheel unit as shown. Make 160.

Make 160.

3 Arrange four matching half-square-triangle units, four muslin rectangles, and one pinwheel unit from step 2 as shown. Sew the units and rectangles together into rows, and then join the rows. Make 160 blocks.

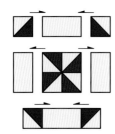 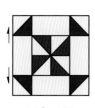

Make 160.

## Making the Half Blocks

For each block, you'll need the following pieces:

**Assorted print:** Two 2¼" quarter-square triangles and one 1⅞" half-square triangle

**Coordinating print:** Two 1⅞" half-square triangles

**Muslin:** Two 2¼" quarter-square triangles, three 1⅞" half-square triangles, and two rectangles

1 Sew one print quarter-square triangle and one muslin quarter-square triangle together along one short edge as shown; press. Make one and one reversed.

Make 1 of each.

2 Sew together a muslin half-square triangle and a coordinating print half-square triangle to make unit A. Using the print that matches the units in step 1, sew the print half-square triangle to a muslin half-square triangle to make unit B.

Unit A     Unit B

3 Using the print that matches unit A, sew a print half-square triangle and a muslin half-square triangle to adjacent sides of unit A as shown.

4 Lay out the unit from step 3, the two units from step 1, unit B from step 2, and two muslin rectangles as shown. Sew the pieces together into rows, and then join the rows to complete the block. Repeat to make a total of 10 half blocks.

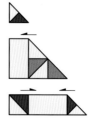 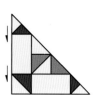

Make 10.

# Assembling the Quilt Top

1  Sew purple 3¾" half-square triangles to adjacent sides of a block as shown. Sew a purple 7" quarter-square triangle to the unit. Make 12.

Make 12.

2  Sew purple 7" quarter-square triangles to opposite sides of a block as shown. Make 78.

 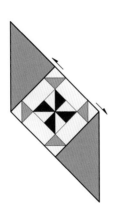

Make 78.

3  Sew together two units from step 1 and 13 units from step 2 to make a row. This is row 1. Repeat to make six rows.

Make 6.

4 Sew a purple 7" quarter-square triangle to a half block as shown. Make 10.

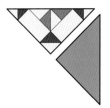 

Make 10.

5 Sew purple quarter-square triangles to opposite sides of a block as shown. Make 70.

 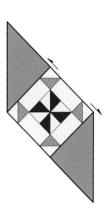

Make 70.

6 Sew together two half-block units from step 4 and 14 block units from step 5 to make a row. This is row 2. Repeat to make five rows.

Make 5.

7 Fold the purple triangles in half and pin-mark the centers. Pin a row 1 to a row 2, matching the pins to the points of the blocks. Sew the rows together. Continue in this manner until all of the rows are joined.

## Finishing the Quilt

Refer to "Finishing Techniques" on page 236 for details on the following steps.

1 Layer and baste your quilt, and quilt as desired.

2 Using the 1¾"-wide binding strips and referring to "Single-Fold Binding" on page 239, prepare and attach the binding.

Quilt assembly

# Soldier's Cot Quilt

**FINISHED QUILT:** 54" × 79" • **FINISHED BLOCK:** 12½" × 12½"

*Designed and pieced by Kathleen Tracy; quilted by Dawn Larsen*

*Women volunteers worked hard to improve the horrible conditions at hospitals and military camps during the Civil War. Cot-sized quilts, similar to this reproduction, were particularly in demand. Of more than 250,000 quilts made for Union soldiers, only a few exist today.*

## Materials

*Yardage is based on 42"-wide fabric.*

15 scraps, 12" × 12", of reproduction prints for block
  backgrounds
15 scraps, 3" × 3", of reproduction prints for
  block centers
15 reproduction prints, ⅛ yard each, for block Xs
½ yard of teal print for inner border
2 yards of brown print for outer border
⅝ yard of dark blue print for binding
4⅞ yards of fabric for backing
60" × 85" piece of batting
15" square ruler

## Cutting

*All measurements include ¼"-wide seam allowances.*

**From *each* of the 15 assorted prints for block backgrounds, cut:**

1 square, 11" × 11"; cut the square into quarters
  diagonally to yield 4 triangles (60 total)

**From *each* of the 15 assorted prints for block centers, cut:**

1 square, 2⅝" × 2⅝" (15 total)

**From *each* of the 15 assorted prints for block Xs, cut:**

1 strip, 2⅝" × 42"; cut into 4 rectangles, 2⅝" × 9" (60
  total)

**From the teal print, cut:**

6 strips, 2½" × 42"

**From the brown print, cut on the *lengthwise* grain:**

2 strips, 6½" × 54"
2 strips, 6½" × 67"

**From the dark blue print, cut:**

7 strips, 2½" × 42"

## Making the Blocks

For each X block, choose four matching 2⅝" × 9" rectangles, four matching triangles for the background, and a 2⅝" square for the center. Press the seam allowances as indicated by the arrows, or as otherwise instructed.

1 Sew a triangle to each side of a 2⅝" × 9" rectangle. Make two units.

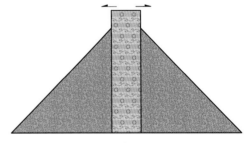

Make 2.

2 Sew the remaining two 2⅝" × 9" rectangles to opposite sides of a 2⅝" square.

3 Sew the two units from step 1 together with the unit from step 2 as shown. Referring to "Pressing Pointers" at right, press the seam allowances as desired.

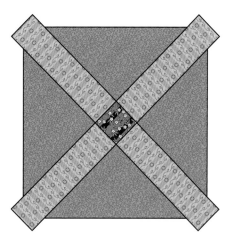

4 Place the 6½" point of a square ruler in the center of the block. Trim the sides of the block. Rotate the block 180° and trim to 13" square, including seam allowances. Make a total of 15 blocks.

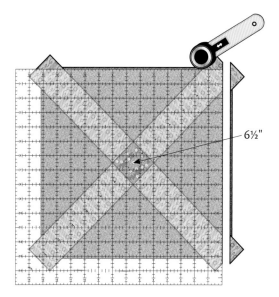

6½"

## PRESSING POINTERS

You may want to press the seam allowances open for these blocks to make quilt-top assembly easier. Sew with a shorter stitch length if you choose this option. You can also press the seam allowances of seven of the blocks in the opposite direction so that the seams will butt together. This will limit your ability to juggle blocks around in the final arrangement, but the seams will be easy to match.

## Assembling the Quilt Top

1 Lay out the blocks in five rows of three blocks each as shown.

2 Sew the blocks together into rows, pressing the seam allowances in opposite directions from row to row. Sew the rows together and press the seam allowances in one direction.

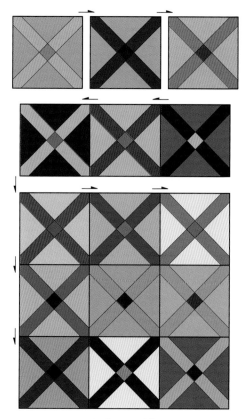

Quilt assembly

3 Sew the teal 2½" × 42" strips together end to end. Cut two strips, 2½" × 63", and sew them to the sides of the quilt top. Press the seam allowances toward the borders. Cut the remainder of the pieced strip into two strips, 2½" × 42", and sew them to the top and bottom of the quilt top. Press the seam allowances toward the borders.

4 Sew the brown 6½" × 67" strips to the sides of the quilt top, and then add the brown 6½" × 54" strips to the top and bottom.

## Finishing the Quilt

Refer to "Finishing Techniques" on page 236 for details on the following steps.

1 Layer and baste your quilt, and quilt as desired.

2 Using the dark blue 2½"-wide strips, prepare and attach the binding.

Adding borders

# Hard Crackers

**FINISHED QUILT:** 17⅛" × 19¼" • **FINISHED BLOCK:** 2⅛" × 2⅛"

*Designed and pieced by Carol Hopkins; quilted by Lisa Ramsey*

*Besides giving the historical name to this scrappy quilt block, crackers were a food staple for Civil War soldiers. The dried wafers were shipped to troops from Northern factories, a process that could take months. The hard crackers proved nearly indestructible—and barely palatable.*

## Materials

Yardage is based on 42"-wide fabric.

120 scraps, at least 3" × 3", of assorted dark prints for blocks

60 scraps, at least 3" × 3", of assorted light prints for blocks

30 scraps, at least 1½" × 2½", of assorted medium prints for blocks

¼ yard of red print for inner border

⅝ yard of brown stripe OR ⅜ yard of nondirectional print for outer border

¼ yard of brown print for binding

¾ yard of fabric for backing

23" × 25" piece of batting

## Cutting

All measurements include ¼"-wide seam allowances.

**From the dark scraps, cut:**
60 squares, 2½" × 2½"; cut the squares in half diagonally to yield 120 triangles (60 are extra*)
60 rectangles, 1" × 2"

**From the light scraps, cut:**
60 squares, 2½" × 2½"; cut the squares in half diagonally to yield 120 triangles (60 are extra*)

**From the medium scraps, cut:**
30 rectangles, 1" × 2"

**From the red print, cut:**
2 strips, 1" × 42"; crosscut into 4 strips, 1" × 21"

**From the brown stripe, cut on the *lengthwise* grain:** \*\*
4 strips, 3¼" × 20"

**From the brown print, cut:**
3 strips, 2" × 42"

*\*To avoid cutting extra triangles, cut just 30 squares each of the dark and light prints and then cut them in half diagonally to yield 60 triangles of each value. However, your quilt will not be as scrappy as the sample.*

*\*\*If you are using a nondirectional print, cut 2 strips, 3¼" × 42", across the fabric width; crosscut each strip into 2 strips, 3¼" × 20".*

## Making the Blocks

Each Cracker block is made from seven different fabrics—two dark rectangles, one medium rectangle, two light triangles, and two dark triangles. The triangles are cut larger than needed and trimmed to size after the block is constructed. Instructions are for making one block. Press the seam allowances as indicated by the arrows, or as otherwise instructed.

1 Sew three rectangles together in a dark, medium, dark sequence.

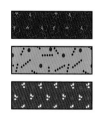 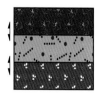

2 Sew dark triangles to opposite ends of the unit, positioning the triangles across the seamed ends of the unit.

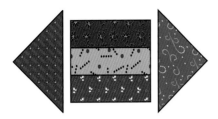

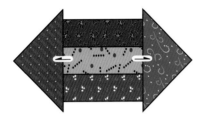

3 Sew light triangles to the top and bottom of the unit.

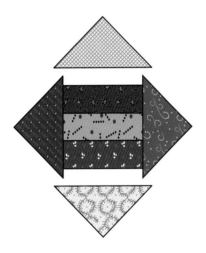

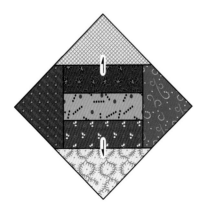

4 Leaving ¼" for seam allowance on all sides of the block, trim the excess triangle fabric so that the block measures 2⅝" square, including seam allowances. Make 30 blocks.

## Assembling the Quilt Top

1 Arrange the Cracker blocks in six rows of five blocks each.

2 Sew the blocks together into rows, and then join the rows.

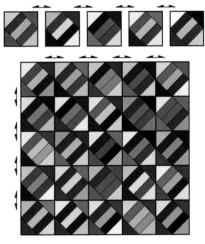

Quilt assembly

3 Measure the length of the quilt top through the center and trim two red 1"-wide strips to this measurement. Sew the strips to the sides of the quilt top. Measure the width of the quilt top through the center, including the borders just added. Trim the remaining red strips to this measurement and sew them to the top and bottom of the quilt top.

4 Measure the length of the quilt top through the center and trim two striped 3¼"-wide strips to this measurement. Sew the strips to the sides of the quilt top. Measure the width of the quilt top through the center, including the borders just added. Trim the remaining striped strips to this measurement and sew them to the top and bottom of the quilt top.

## Finishing the Quilt

Refer to "Finishing Techniques" on page 236 for details on the following steps.

1 Layer and baste your quilt, and quilt as desired.

2 Using the brown print 2"-wide strips, prepare and attach the binding.

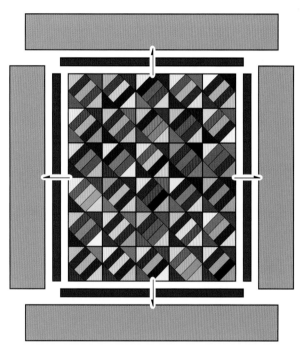

Adding borders

# Sadie's Quilt

**FINISHED QUILT:** 22¼" × 26" • **FINISHED BLOCK:** 3" × 3"

*Designed and made by Jo Morton*

*Easy-to-piece small blocks in a cozy mix of prints create the perfect autumn accent, and the lack of a border makes the quilt even quicker to finish. Combine it with fall decorations or rustic antiques for a heartwarming seasonal display.*

## Materials

*Yardage is based on 42"-wide fabric. Fat quarters are 18" × 21"; fat eighths are 9" × 21".*

30 fat eighths OR scraps of assorted black prints for blocks

30 fat eighths OR scraps of assorted orange prints for blocks

⅓ yard of tan print for setting squares

¼ yard of gray print for setting triangles

1 fat quarter OR ¼ yard of black print for binding

¾ yard of fabric for backing

27" × 30" piece of batting

## Cutting

*All measurements include ¼"-wide seam allowances. For each block, use one black and one orange print. Keep the matching pieces together as you cut for easy piecing.*

**From *each* of the 30 assorted black prints, cut:**

4 squares, 1¼" × 1¼" (120 total)

1 square, 2" × 2" (30 total)

**From *each* of the 30 assorted orange prints, cut:**

4 rectangles, 1¼" × 2" (120 total)

**From the tan print, cut:**

20 squares, 3½" × 3½"

**From the gray print, cut:**

5 squares, 5¾" × 5¾"; cut the squares into quarters diagonally to yield 20 triangles (2 are extra)

2 squares, 3¼" × 3¼"; cut the squares in half diagonally to yield 4 triangles

**From the black print for binding, cut:**

4 strips, 1⅛" × 21"

### MIX-AND-MATCH FABRICS

Although the cutting list gives you what you need for one block at a time, Jo Morton prefers to cut lots of pieces, and then lay out the blocks to be sure she likes them. If any of your planned combinations don't seem to work, cut new pieces so you can mix and match fabrics until you're satisfied. You may also want to audition your blocks on two or three different background fabrics (for the setting squares, setting triangles, and corner triangles) before you decide which ones to use. As Jo says, don't be afraid to experiment—and change your mind!

## Making the Blocks

Press the seam allowances as indicated by the arrows, or as otherwise instructed.

1. Arrange four 1¼" squares and one 2" square from one black print along with four 1¼" × 2" rectangles from one orange print in three rows.

2. Sew the pieces in each row together.

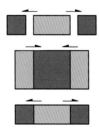

3 Sew the rows together, matching the seam intersections, to complete the Uneven Nine Patch block.

4 Repeat steps 1–3 to make 30 blocks.

## Assembling the Quilt Top

1 Lay out the blocks, tan setting squares, and gray setting triangles in diagonal rows as shown in the quilt assembly diagram below.

2 Sew the pieces together into rows, and then join the rows, matching seam intersections. Add the corner triangles last.

3 Trim and square the quilt edges, leaving a ¼" seam allowance beyond the points of the blocks.

## Finishing the Quilt

Refer to "Finishing Techniques" on page 236 for details on the following steps.

1 Layer and baste your quilt, and quilt as desired.

2 Using the black 1⅛"-wide strips and referring to "Single-Fold Binding" on page 239, prepare and attach the binding.

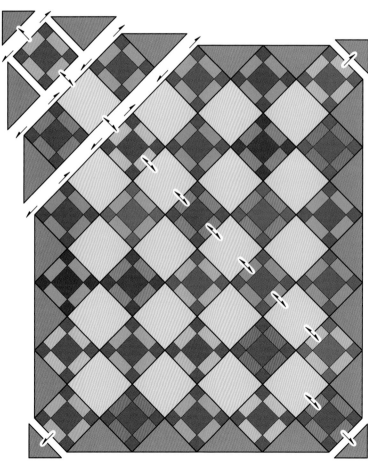

Quilt assembly

# Album Quilt

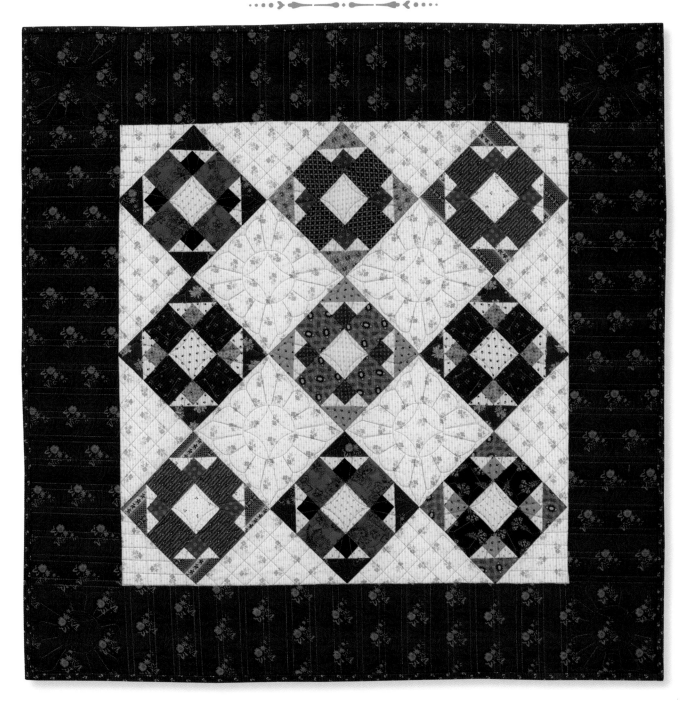

**FINISHED QUILT:** 36" × 36" • **FINISHED BLOCK:** 6" × 6"

*Designed and pieced by Kathleen Tracy; quilted by Dawn Larsen*

*Album quilts from the 19th century sometimes displayed favorite quotes or even political statements. For a sweetly personalized friendship quilt, write the names of special people in the light squares with a fine-point permanent marking pen.*

## Materials

*Yardage is based on 42"-wide fabric.*

⅜ yard *total* of assorted light prints for blocks

⅝ yard *total* of assorted medium and dark prints for blocks

⅝ yard of light shirting print for setting blocks and triangles

¾ yard of red print for border

⅜ yard of dark blue print for binding

1⅓ yards of fabric for backing

42" × 42" piece of batting

## Cutting

*All measurements include ¼"-wide seam allowances.*

### BLOCKS

*Cutting is for 1 block. You'll need 9 total.*

**From 1 light print, cut:**

1 square, 2½" × 2½"

4 squares, 1⅞" × 1⅞"; cut the squares in half diagonally to yield 8 triangles

**From 1 medium or dark print, cut:**

4 squares, 2½" × 2½"

**From a second medium or dark print, cut:**

2 squares, 2⅞" × 2⅞"; cut the squares in half diagonally to yield 4 triangles

**From a third medium or dark print, cut:**

4 squares, 1½" × 1½"

### SETTING PIECES, BORDER, AND BINDING

**From the light shirting print, cut:**

4 squares, 6½" × 6½"

2 squares, 9¾" × 9¾"; cut the squares into quarters diagonally to yield 8 triangles

2 squares, 5⅛" × 5⅛"; cut the squares in half diagonally to yield 4 triangles

**From the red print, cut:**

2 strips, 5½" × 26"

2 strips, 5½" × 36"

**From the dark blue print, cut:**

4 strips, 2½" × 42"

## Making the Blocks

The directions are written for making one block at a time. Press the seam allowances as indicated by the arrows, or as otherwise instructed.

1 Sew two matching light 1⅞" triangles to adjacent sides of a medium or dark 1½" square. Make four.

Make 4.

2 Sew a medium or dark 2⅞" triangle to the long edge of each unit from step 1.

Make 4.

3 Sew the units from step 2, four medium or dark 2½" squares, and a light 2½" square into rows as shown. Join the rows to complete the block.

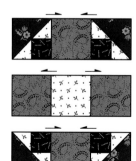 

4 Repeat steps 1–3 to make a total of nine blocks.

### SIGNING MADE EASY

If you plan to invite people to sign your quilt, make it easier by stabilizing the fabric with freezer paper. Cut the freezer paper into pieces that will fit behind the light setting squares and triangles and iron, shiny side down, to the back of the light fabric. Use a fine-point permanent marker for the signatures. Gently remove the freezer paper before sewing the quilt top together.

## Assembling the Quilt Top

1 Lay out the blocks and light shirting squares and setting triangles in diagonal rows.

2 Sew the pieces together into rows; press. Sew the rows together, pressing the seam allowances in opposite directions. Add the corner setting triangles last and press.

Quilt assembly

3 Sew the red 5½" × 26" strips to the sides of the quilt top, and then add the red 5½" × 36" strips to the top and bottom.

Adding borders

## Finishing the Quilt

Refer to "Finishing Techniques" on page 236 for details on the following steps.

1 Layer and baste your quilt, and quilt as desired.

2 Using the dark blue 2½"-wide strips, prepare and attach the binding.

# Flying North

**FINISHED QUILT:** 66⅞" × 81¾" • **FINISHED BLOCK:** 10½" × 10½"

*Designed and made by Julie Hendricksen*

*An intricate horizontal zigzag setting revs up this design featuring Shoofly variation blocks. Notice that to create the chevron effect, you need to make half blocks to start and end alternate rows—a little extra effort, but well worth it!*

## Materials

*Yardage is based on 42"-wide fabric. Fat eighths are 9" × 21".*

11 fat eighths of assorted light prints for blocks (each print will yield 2 blocks)

22 fat eighths of assorted dark prints for blocks (each print will be used twice)

4 yards of navy print for setting triangles and border

⅔ yard of light print for binding

5 yards of fabric for backing

74" × 89" piece of batting

## Cutting

*All measurements include ¼"-wide seam allowances.*

### From *each* of the 11 assorted light prints:

1 strip, 4⅜" × 21"; crosscut into 4 squares, 4⅜" × 4⅜". Cut the squares in half diagonally to yield 8 triangles (88 total).

2 strips, 2¼" × 2¼"; crosscut into 32 squares, 2¼" × 2¼" (352 total)

### From *each* of the 22 assorted dark prints, cut:

1 strip, 4⅜" × 21"; crosscut into 2 squares, 4⅜" × 4⅜". Cut the squares in half diagonally to yield 4 triangles (88 total).

1 square, 4" × 4" (22 total)

1 strip, 4" × 21"; crosscut into 8 rectangles, 2¼" × 4" (176 total)

### From the navy print, cut:

5 strips, 16¼" × 42"; crosscut into 9 squares, 16¼" × 16¼". Cut the squares into quarters diagonally to yield 36 triangles (2 are extra).

2 strips, 8½" × 42"; crosscut into 6 squares, 8½" × 8½". Cut the squares in half diagonally to yield 12 corner triangles.

8 strips, 4" × 42"

### From the light print for binding, cut:

8 strips, 2½" × 42"

## Making the Blocks

For each block, use one light print and two different dark prints—one for the flying-geese units and one for the triangle squares and center square. It's easiest to audition the fabrics first and decide on all the combinations before you begin assembling the blocks. Press the seam allowances as indicated by the arrows, or as otherwise instructed.

1 Draw a diagonal line from corner to corner on the wrong side of a light 2¼" square. Place the marked square on one end of a dark 2¼" × 4" rectangle, right sides together and corners aligned. Sew on the drawn line. Trim the excess fabric, leaving ¼" seam allowances, and press. Repeat on the other end of the rectangle to complete a flying-geese unit. Make a total of eight matching units.

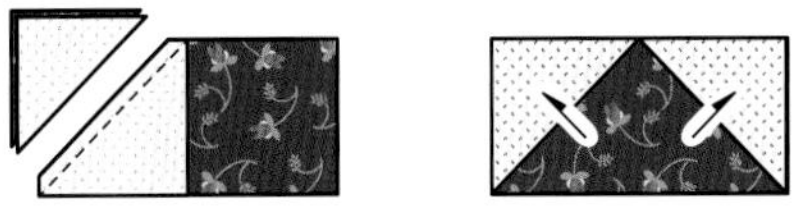

Make 8.

2 With right sides facing, sew together a light 4⅜" triangle and a dark 4⅜" triangle (different from the dark print used in step 1). The unit should measure 4" square, including seam allowances. Repeat to make a total of four matching half-square-triangle units.

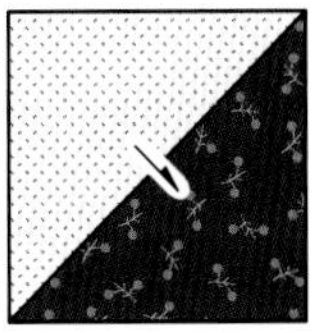

Make 4.

3 Arrange the eight flying-geese units, the four half-square-triangle units, and a dark 4" square that matches the half-square-triangle units, as shown. Sew the pieces together into rows, and then join the rows to complete the block. The block should measure 11" square, including seam allowances. Repeat to make 22 blocks.

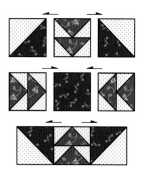 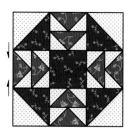

Make 22.

## Assembling the Quilt Top

1 Lay out the blocks and setting triangles in five rows. The first, third, and fifth rows consist of four blocks each. The second and fourth rows contain five blocks each, but the blocks on the ends will be trimmed to half blocks in the next step. Sew the blocks and triangles together into rows, pressing the seam allowances toward the setting triangles.

2 Trim the second and fourth rows, leaving a ¼" seam allowance outside the seam intersections.

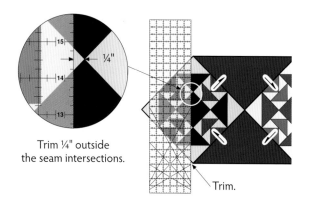

Trim ¼" outside the seam intersections.

Trim.

3 Join the rows to complete the quilt center.

4 Sew the navy 4" × 42" strips in pairs end to end to make four long strips. Measure the length of the quilt top through the center. Trim two strips to this measurement and sew them to the sides of the quilt top. Measure the width of the quilt top through the center, including the borders just added. Trim the remaining pieced strips to this measurement and sew them to the top and bottom of the quilt top.

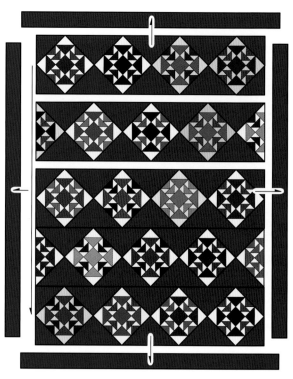

Quilt assembly

## Finishing the Quilt

Refer to "Finishing Techniques" on page 236 for details on the following steps.

1 Layer and baste your quilt, and quilt as desired.

2 Using the light 2½"-wide strips, prepare and attach the binding.

# Fruit Pie

**FINISHED QUILT:** 30½" × 30½" • **FINISHED BLOCK:** 3" × 3"

*Designed and made by Mary Etherington and Connie Tesene*

*One hundred blocks line up in an orderly straight-row setting, while their design sparkles with diagonal movement. This block goes by several names, but the sweetest sounding is Fruit Pie, cooling on a windowsill in anticipation of a loved one's return.*

## Materials

*Yardage is based on 42"-wide fabric.*
¼ yard *total* of assorted white prints for blocks
12 assorted blue prints, ¼ yard each, for blocks
12 assorted red prints, ¼ yard each, for blocks
¼ yard of dark blue print for binding
1 yard of fabric for backing
34" × 34" piece of batting

## Cutting

*All measurements include ¼"-wide seam allowances.*

**From the assorted white prints, cut:**
88 squares, 1⅞" × 1⅞"; cut the squares in half
    diagonally to yield 176 triangles

**From the assorted blue prints, cut:**
180 squares, 1½" × 1½"
60 squares, 2⅞" × 2⅞"; cut the squares in half
    diagonally to yield 120 triangles

**From the assorted red prints, cut:**
120 squares, 1½" × 1½"
40 squares, 2⅞" × 2⅞"; cut the squares in half
    diagonally to yield 80 triangles
112 squares, 1⅞" × 1⅞"; cut the squares in half
    diagonally to yield 224 triangles

**From the dark blue print, cut:**
4 strips, 2¼" × 42"

## Making the Blocks

All 100 blocks in this quilt are assembled the same way; only the color placement changes. You'll need four blue-and-white blocks for the quilt center, 40 red-and-white blocks for the second and fourth rounds, and 56 blue-and-red blocks for the remainder of the quilt. Press the seam allowances as indicated by the arrows, or as otherwise instructed.

### BLUE-AND-WHITE BLOCKS

1 Sew a white 1⅞" triangle to the right edge of a blue 1½" square. Make two matching units.

Make 2.

2 Sew white 1⅞" triangles to opposite sides of a matching blue 1½" square. The bias side of one triangle (the long diagonal edge) should be facing up and the bias side of the second triangle should be facing down as shown.

Make 1.

3 Sew the units from step 1 to the top and bottom of the unit from step 2, matching seam intersections.

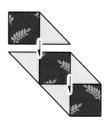

4 Sew a matching blue 2⅞" triangle to each side of the unit from step 3. Be careful not to stretch the bias edges when stitching and pressing. The block should measure 3½" square, including seam allowances. Make four blue-and-white blocks.

Make 4.

## RED-AND-WHITE BLOCKS

These blocks are made exactly like the blue-and-white blocks, except you'll replace the blue triangles and squares with red ones. Make 40 red-and-white blocks.

Make 40.

## BLUE-AND-RED BLOCKS

Again, these blocks are made in the same manner as the other blocks. For each block, you'll use three blue 1½" squares, two blue 2⅞" triangles, and four red 1⅞" triangles. Make 56 blue-and-red blocks.

Make 56.

## Assembling the Quilt Top

1 Following the quilt plan below for color placement and block orientation, arrange the blocks into 10 rows of 10 blocks each.

2 Sew the blocks together into rows, pressing the seam allowances in opposite directions from row to row. Then join the rows, matching points carefully. Press the seam allowances in one direction.

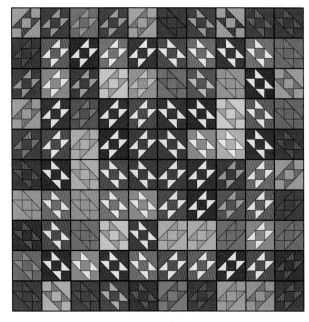

Quilt plan

## Finishing the Quilt

Refer to "Finishing Techniques" on page 236 for details on the following steps.

1 Layer and baste your quilt, and quilt as desired.

2 Using the dark blue 2¼"-wide strips, prepare and attach the binding.

# Plantation Road

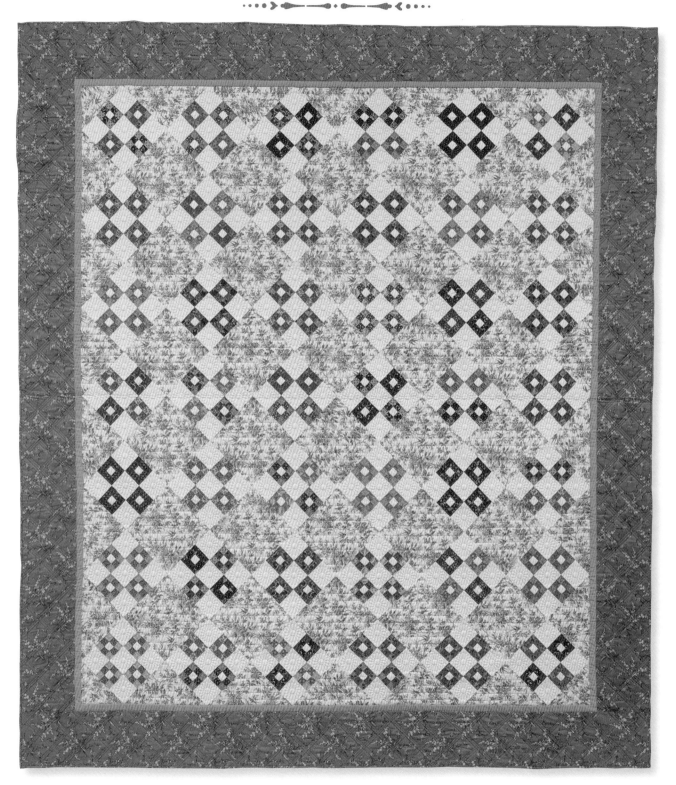

**FINISHED QUILT:** 95" × 107½" • **FINISHED BLOCK:** 9" × 9"

*Designed by Paula Barnes; pieced by Mary Ellen Robison;*
*quilted by Marcella Pickett and Margie Love of Crooked Creek Quilts*

*Many quilts made with reproduction prints convey a somber reverence for history, and rightfully so. These on-point squares of red toile, however, dance with Double Nine Patch blocks as a reminder that beauty and elegance endure in even the darkest of times.*

## Materials

*Yardage is based on 42"-wide fabric. Fat quarters are 18" × 21".*

2½ yards of cream tone on tone or solid for pieced blocks

14 assorted brown prints, ¼ yard OR 1 fat quarter each, for pieced blocks

14 assorted medium prints, ¼ yard OR 1 fat quarter each, in teal, red, pink, and tan for pieced blocks

3½ yards of red toile for alternate blocks and setting triangles

½ yard of pink print for inner border

2¾ yards of dark large-scale floral for outer border

1 yard of fabric for binding

9 yards of fabric for backing

103" × 116" piece of batting

## Cutting

*All measurements include ¼"-wide seam allowances.*

**From the cream tone on tone, cut:**

19 strips, 3½" × 42"; crosscut into 210 squares, 3½" × 3½"

9 strips, 1½" × 42"; crosscut into 42 rectangles, 1½" × 7"

**From *each* of the 14 assorted brown prints, cut:**

12 rectangles, 1½" × 7" (168 total)

**From *each* of the 14 assorted medium prints, cut:**

12 rectangles, 1½" × 7" (168 total)

**From the red toile, cut:**

6 squares, 14" × 14"; cut the squares into quarters diagonally to yield 24 triangles (2 are extra)

30 squares, 9½" × 9½"

2 squares, 7¼" × 7¼"; cut the squares in half diagonally to yield 4 triangles

**From the pink print, cut:**

9 strips, 1½" × 42"

**From the dark large-scale floral, cut on the *lengthwise* grain:**

2 strips, 8½" × 91½"

2 strips, 8½" × 95"

**From the binding fabric, cut:**

11 strips, 1⅞" × 42", or bias strips to total 440"

## Making the Blocks

Press the seam allowances as indicated by the arrows, or as otherwise instructed.

1 Sew two matching medium 1½" × 7" rectangles and one brown 1½" × 7" rectangle together to make a strip set. Make two matching strip sets. Cut four segments, 1½" wide, from each strip set for a total of eight segments.

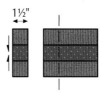

1½"

Make 2 strip sets.
Cut 8 segments.

2 Using the same brown print used in step 1, sew two brown 1½" × 7" rectangles to a cream 1½" × 7" rectangle. Cut four segments, 1½" wide.

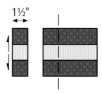

1½"

Make 1 strip set.
Cut 4 segments.

3 Sew the segments from steps 1 and 2 together to make four identical nine-patch units.

Make 4.

4 Sew the nine-patch units together with five cream 3½" squares to make the Double Nine Patch block.

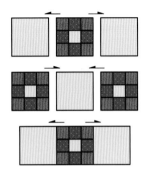 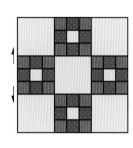

5 Repeat steps 1–4 to make a total of 42 blocks. Note that some blocks include nine-patch units in two different color schemes. Make several nine-patch units, and then combine them with others when assembling the Double Nine Patch blocks.

## Assembling the Quilt Top

1 Referring to the assembly diagram below, lay out the blocks and red-toile squares and triangles in diagonal rows, with six blocks across and seven blocks down. Rearrange the Double Nine Patch blocks until you are pleased with the color placement.

2 Sew the pieces together into diagonal rows, and then join the rows. Add the corner triangles last.

3 Trim the selvages from the pink 1½" × 42" strips and sew the strips together end to end. Press the seam allowances to one side. From this strip

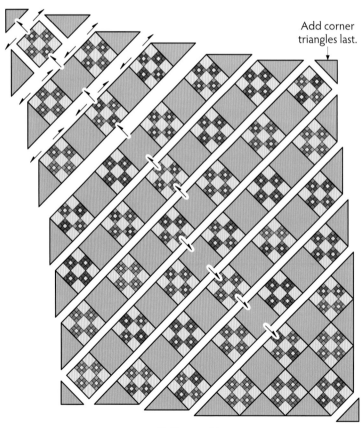

Add corner triangles last.

Quilt assembly

cut two strips, 89½" long, for the side borders and two strips, 79" long, for the top and bottom borders. Sew the side borders to the quilt top first, and then add the top and bottom borders.

4 Sew the floral 8½" × 91½" strips to the sides of the quilt top, and then add the floral 8½" × 95" strips to the top and bottom.

## Finishing the Quilt

Refer to "Finishing Techniques" on page 236 for details on the following steps.

1 Layer and baste your quilt, and quilt as desired.

2 Using the 1⅞"-wide binding strips, prepare and attach the binding.

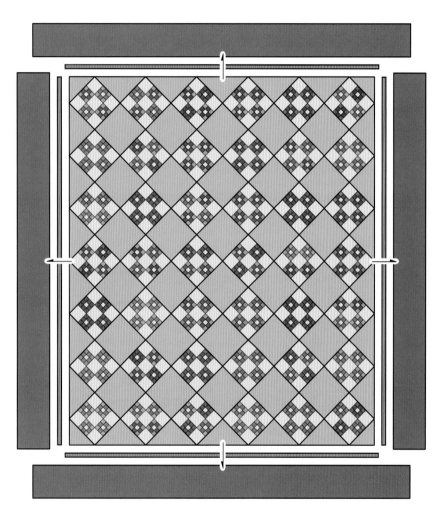

Adding borders

# Homeward Bound

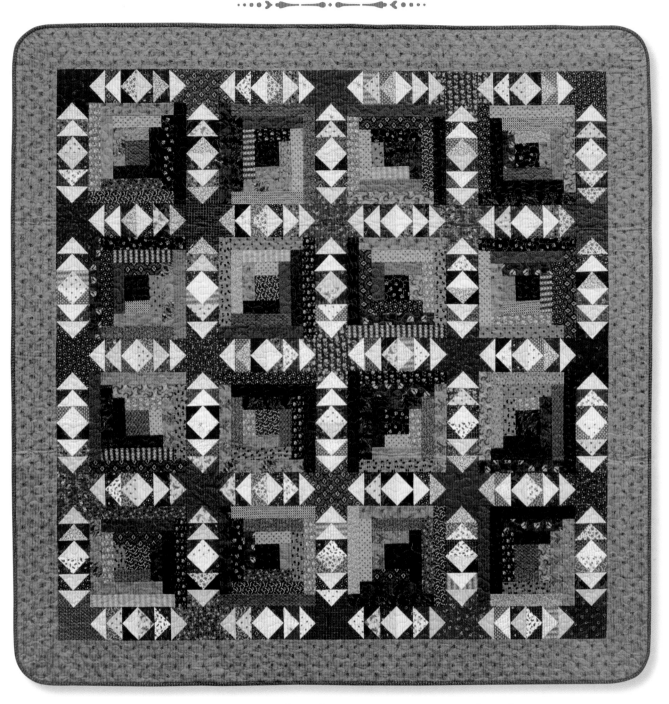

**FINISHED QUILT:** 78" × 78" • **FINISHED BLOCK:** 12" × 12"

*Designed and made by Evelyn Sloppy*

*Two easy and familiar blocks, Log Cabin and Flying Geese, are stitched in wonderful blues, reds, and golds to exude comfort and charm. Although the geese travel in many directions, the pleasure of a warm landing place is never far away.*

## Materials

*Yardage is based on 42"-wide fabric. Fat quarters are 18" × 21".*

2 yards *total* OR 8 fat quarters of assorted blue prints for Log Cabin blocks

1½ yards *total* OR 6 fat quarters of assorted gold prints for Log Cabin blocks

1¾ yards *total* OR 7 fat quarters of assorted cream prints for Flying Geese blocks

2½ yards *total* OR 10 fat quarters of assorted red prints for Flying Geese blocks

1⅝ yards of gold print for border

¾ yard of fabric for binding

5 yards of fabric for backing

82" × 82" piece of batting

## Cutting

*All measurements include ¼"-wide seam allowances.*

**From the assorted blue prints, cut a *total* of:**

16 squares, 3½" × 3½"

Cut the remaining prints into 2"-wide strips (the equivalent of at least 25 strips, 42" long); crosscut into the following:

- 16 rectangles, 2" × 5"
- 16 rectangles, 2" × 6½"
- 16 rectangles, 2" × 8"
- 16 rectangles, 2" × 9½"
- 16 rectangles, 2" × 11"
- 16 rectangles, 2" × 12½"

**From the assorted gold prints, cut:**

2"-wide strips (the equivalent of at least 21 strips, 42" long); crosscut into the following:

- 16 rectangles, 2" × 3½"
- 16 rectangles, 2" × 5"
- 16 rectangles, 2" × 6½"
- 16 rectangles, 2" × 8"
- 16 rectangles, 2" × 9½"
- 16 rectangles, 2" × 11"

**From the assorted cream prints, cut a *total* of:**

60 squares, 5½" × 5½"

**From the assorted red prints, cut a *total* of:**

25 squares, 4½" × 4½"

240 squares, 3" × 3"

**From the gold print for border, cut:**

9 strips, 5½" × 42"

**From the binding fabric, cut:**

9 strips, 2½" × 42", or bias strips to total 322"

## Making the Blocks

Press the seam allowances as indicated by the arrows, or as otherwise instructed.

Starting with a blue 3½" square, add the blue and gold 2"-wide strips one at a time, in the numbered order shown. Press all seam allowances toward the outside. The block should measure 12½" square, including seam allowances. Make 16 blocks.

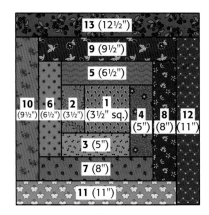

Make 16.

## Making the Sashing Units

1 Draw a diagonal line from corner to corner on the wrong side of the red 3" squares. Align two marked squares on opposite corners of a cream 5½" square, right sides together. The squares will overlap in the center and the drawn lines will connect. Sew ¼" from both sides of the lines. Cut apart on the drawn lines and press. Place a marked red square on the corner of the large triangle of each unit, right sides together. Make sure the drawn diagonal line starts at the corner and ends at the center. Sew ¼" from both sides of the line. Cut apart on the drawn line and press. Make a total of 240 Flying Geese blocks. Trim the blocks to measure 2½" × 4½", including seam allowances.

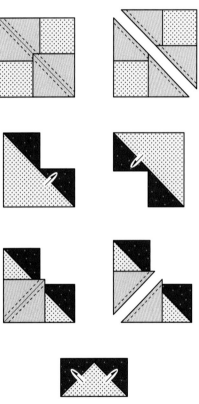

Make 240.

2 Lay out the Log Cabin blocks, Flying Geese blocks, and red 4½" squares as shown. Place four matching Flying Geese blocks around a matching red 4½" square to make a star. Around the outer edges, you will need only three matching Flying Geese blocks for each red 4½" square and two matching Flying Geese blocks for the red squares in the corners. Place the rest of the Flying Geese blocks randomly.

3 Once you determine the arrangement of your quilt, sew the six Flying Geese blocks together for each sashing section as shown.

Press open or to either side.

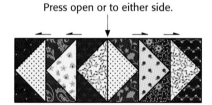

## Assembling the Quilt Top

1 Sew the blocks, sashing, and red 4½" squares together into rows. Join the rows.

2 Sew the gold 5½"-wide strips together end to end and use this long pieced strip to prepare and add a mitered border. Visit ShopMartingale.com/HowtoQuilt if you would like illustrated instructions about mitering a border.

## Finishing the Quilt

Refer to "Finishing Techniques" on page 236 for details on the following steps.

1 Layer and baste your quilt, and quilt as desired.

2 To make the quilt with rounded corners as shown in the photo on page 148, simply trim the corners using a dinner plate as a guide. Then use 2½"-wide bias strips to prepare and attach the binding. If you would like to leave the corners of the quilt square, you can use 2½"-wide straight-grain strips to bind the quilt.

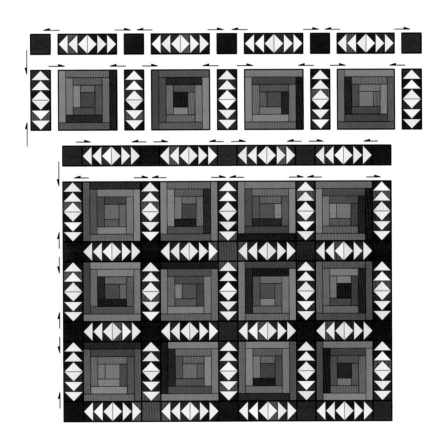

# Friday Night Special

**FINISHED QUILT:** 69½" × 81½" • **FINISHED BLOCK:** 8½" × 8½"

*Designed and made by Gayle Bong*

*The Chimney Sweep block may become one of your favorites after you see it made up in a few of your favorite fabrics. If you're short on scraps, substitute 2½ yards of just one fabric for the scrappy alternate squares and setting triangles.*

## Materials

*Yardage is based on 42"-wide fabric.*

4⅜ yards *total* of assorted dark scraps for blocks, setting squares, and setting triangles

2⅛ yards of muslin for blocks and inner border

1½ yards of blue print for outer border and binding

5½ yards of fabric for backing

78" × 90" piece of batting

## Cutting

*All measurements include ¼"-wide seam allowances.*

### From the assorted dark scraps, cut:

20 squares, 9" × 9"

2 squares, 8" × 8"; cut the squares in half diagonally to yield 4 triangles

30 strips, 2" × 34"; crosscut each strip into:
- 4 rectangles, 2" × 5" (120 total)
- 8 squares, 2" × 2" (240 total)

Reserve the remainder of the dark scraps for side setting triangles.

### From the muslin, cut:

18 strips, 2" × 42"; crosscut *10 strips* into:
- 120 squares, 2" × 2"; cut *60 squares* in half diagonally to yield 120 triangles
- 30 rectangles, 2" × 5"

9 strips, 3⅜" × 42"; crosscut into 90 squares, 3⅜" × 3⅜". Cut the squares into quarters diagonally to yield 360 triangles.

### From the blue print, cut:

8 strips, 3½" × 42"

8 strips, 2¼" × 42"

### SMART MOVE TO AVOID PROBLEMS

Consider making a sample block to check your seam allowance before cutting the setting squares and triangles. Or, if you have enough scraps, cut the setting squares and triangles after you've made and measured the pieced blocks to find the average size to cut the pieces.

## Making the Blocks

Keep matching fabrics together so one print is used in each block. Press the seam allowances as indicated by the arrows, or as otherwise instructed.

1 Arrange four matching dark squares, two muslin squares, and one muslin rectangle as shown. Sew the squares into rows, and then sew the rows together.

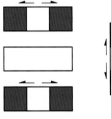

Make 1.

2 Sew a dark square between two large muslin triangles. Sew this unit between a dark rectangle and a small muslin triangle. Make four units. Sew large muslin triangles to opposite ends of the dark rectangle on two of the units.

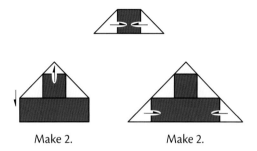

Make 2.          Make 2.

3 Arrange the units from steps 1 and 2 in diagonal rows. Sew the center row together, and then add the corner units to complete the block. Trim the block to 9" square, including seam allowances.

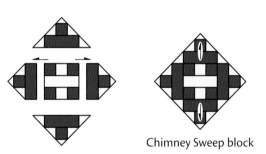

Chimney Sweep block

4 Repeat steps 1–3 to make a total of 30 blocks.

## Assembling the Quilt Top

1 From freezer paper or newspaper, cut a 13¼" square into quarters diagonally to yield four triangles. Using one paper triangle as a template, cut 18 side setting triangles from the remaining dark scraps that you set aside previously.

2 Arrange the Chimney Sweep blocks, dark 9" setting squares, dark side setting triangles, and dark corner setting triangles into diagonal rows.

3 Sew the pieces together into rows, and then join the rows. Add the corner setting triangles last.

Quilt assembly

4 Square up the edges of the quilt top, trimming ¼" past the corners of the blocks.

5 Sew the eight remaining muslin 2"-wide strips together end to end. Measure the width of the quilt top through the center. Cut two strips to this measurement and sew them to the top

and bottom of the quilt top. Press the seam allowances toward the borders. Measure the length of the quilt top through the center, including the borders just added. Cut two strips to this measurement and sew them to the sides of the quilt top to complete the inner border. Press the seam allowances toward the borders.

6 Repeat to add the blue 3½"-wide strips for the outer border.

## Finishing the Quilt

Refer to "Finishing Techniques" on page 236 for details on the following steps.

1 Layer and baste your quilt, and quilt as desired.

2 Using the blue 2¼"-wide strips, prepare and attach the binding.

Adding borders

# Buckwheat Star

**FINISHED QUILT:** 64½" × 64½" • **FINISHED BLOCKS:** 16" × 16" and 4" × 4"

*Designed and made by Mary Etherington and Connie Tesene*

*Nothing says "thrift" like string piecing. Make the most of leftovers or a collection of fat quarters by sewing narrow strips randomly onto foundations to create star points. The effect is dramatic, and you'll feel good about using up and making do.*

## Materials

*Yardage is based on 42"-wide fabric. Fat quarters are 18" × 21".*

25 assorted light, medium, and dark prints, 1 fat quarter each, for blocks

9 assorted cream prints, 1 fat quarter each, for blocks

1⅞ yards of red print for sashing and border

½ yard of dark blue print for binding

4¼ yards of fabric for backing

68" × 68" piece of batting

Foundation-piecing paper or newspaper

## Cutting

*All measurements include ¼"-wide seam allowances.*

**From the assorted light prints, cut:**
32 squares, 1½" × 1½"

**From the assorted dark prints, cut:**
32 squares, 1½" × 1½"

**From the remaining assorted prints, cut:**
170 to 180 strips, 1" to 1½" × 21"*

**From the assorted cream prints, cut:**
9 squares, 7⅞" × 7⅞"; cut the squares into quarters diagonally to yield 36 triangles

9 sets of 4 matching squares, 5¼" × 5¼" (36 total)

**From the red print, cut:**
13 strips, 4½" × 42"; crosscut *6 strips* into 12 rectangles, 4½" × 16½"

**From the dark blue print, cut:**
7 strips, 2¼" × 42"

*\*You may want to cut a few strips of each fabric in various widths, and then cut more strips as needed. The number of strips required will depend on their width and how efficiently you use them.*

### USE SHORT STITCHES
Before you start string piecing onto the foundation paper, adjust your sewing machine to a very short stitch length. The shorter stitches will perforate the foundation paper more effectively than longer stitches and allow for easier paper removal.

## Making the Diamond Units

For complete paper-piecing instructions, visit ShopMartingale.com/HowtoQuilt for free downloadable information.

1. Using the pattern on page 161, trace or photocopy 72 diamonds onto foundation paper or newspaper. If you photocopy the pattern, compare the printed version to the pattern in the book to make sure the size is accurate.

2. Place a fabric strip, right side up, in the approximate center of a diamond foundation, making sure the strip extends at least ½" beyond both sides of the paper.

3. Place a second fabric strip on top of the first strip, right sides together and with the long edges aligned. Make sure the second strip extends at least ½" beyond both sides of the paper. Stitch along the long edge of the strips, using a ¼" seam allowance. Press.

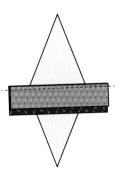

4 Working from the center of the diamond toward each point, continue sewing strips to the foundation paper in the same manner. For added interest, do not line up the strips exactly straight with the previously sewn strip.

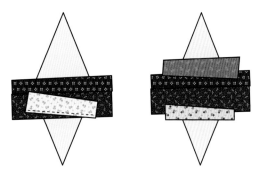

5 When you have completely covered the paper foundation, gently press the diamond unit. Trim the excess fabric ¼" beyond the edge of the paper foundation using a ruler and rotary cutter. Do not remove the paper yet. Repeat to make 72 diamond units.

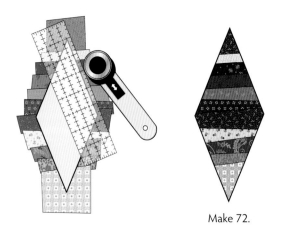

Make 72.

## Making the Star Blocks

Press the seam allowances as indicated by the arrows, or as otherwise instructed.

1 Randomly select two diamond units and place them right sides together. Use pins to match the beginning and ending points on the paper foundation and align the edges of the paper. Pin in place. Starting ¼" from the outer edge of the fabric (exactly at the corner of the paper), backstitch and then stitch along the edge of the paper, sewing the diamonds together to make a quarter-star unit. Make 36 quarter-star units.

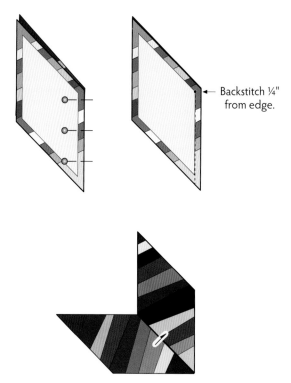

← Backstitch ¼" from edge.

Make 36.

2 Select two quarter-star units and sew them together as instructed in step 1 to make a half-star unit. Make 18 half-star units.

Make 18.

3 Select two half-star units and sew them together in the same manner to make a star unit. Make nine star units.

Make 9.

4 Select four cream squares and four cream triangles, all matching. Place a cream square on top of a diamond unit, right sides together and raw edges aligned. Sew from the outside raw edge to the inside corner, stopping ¼" from the edge with a backstitch.

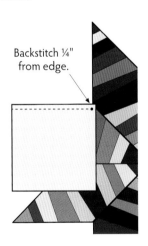

Backstitch ¼" from edge.

5 With right sides together, position the second diamond unit on top of the square so that the raw edges are aligned and the point of the star extends beyond the edge of the square as shown. Sew from the outside edge to the inside corner, stopping at the corner of the paper with a backstitch.

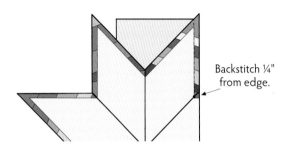

Backstitch ¼" from edge.

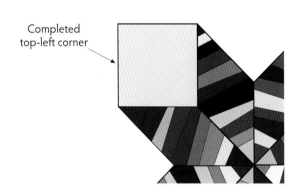

Completed top-left corner

6 Repeat steps 4 and 5, sewing cream squares to the remaining three corners of the star unit. Then sew cream triangles to the sides of the star unit. Press all seam allowances toward the cream squares and triangles. Remove the paper foundations. Make nine Star blocks.

Make 9.

## Making the Checkerboard Blocks

1. Randomly select two light and two dark 1½" squares. Sew them together to make a four-patch unit. Make 16 units.

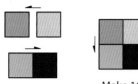

Make 16.

2. Sew four of the assorted four-patch units from step 1 together to make a 16-patch Checkerboard block. The block should measure 4½" square, including seam allowances. Make four blocks.

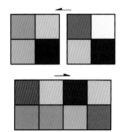
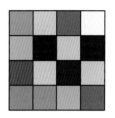

Make 4.

## Assembling the Quilt Top

1. Lay out the Star blocks in three rows of three blocks each, arranging them with the Checkerboard blocks and red sashing rectangles as shown in the quilt assembly diagram at right.

2. Sew the pieces together into rows, and then join the rows. The quilt top should measure 56½" square, including seam allowances.

3. Sew the remaining red 4½"-wide strips together end to end. From the pieced strip, cut two strips, 56½" long, and two strips, 64½" long. Sew the 56½"-long strips to the top and bottom of the quilt top, and then add the 64½"-long strips to the sides.

Quilt assembly

## Finishing the Quilt

Refer to "Finishing Techniques" on page 236 for details on the following steps.

1. Layer and baste your quilt, and quilt as desired.

2. Using the dark blue 2¼"-wide strips, prepare and attach the binding.

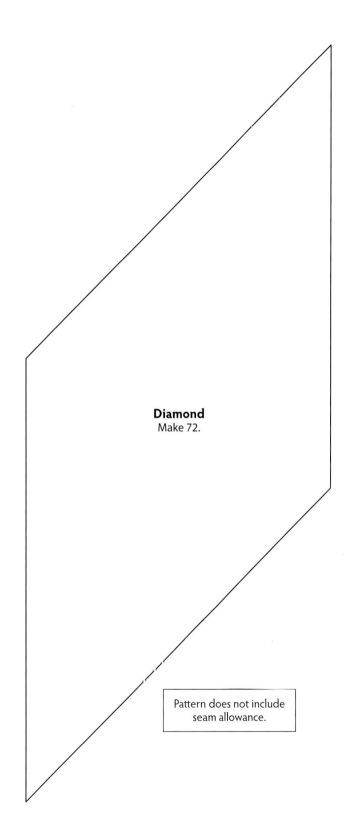

**Diamond**
Make 72.

Pattern does not include
seam allowance.

# Antique Angles

**FINISHED QUILT:** 63" × 76" • **FINISHED BLOCK:** 4½" × 5½"

*Designed and made by Julie Hendricksen*

*This traditional version of a Thousand Pyramids pattern is perfect for using leftovers from other vintage-inspired quilts. The instructions call for fat eighths, but don't hesitate to toss in whatever medium and dark prints are hanging out in your scrap basket.*

## Materials

*Yardage is based on 42"-wide fabric. Fat eighths are 9" × 21".*

46 fat eighths of assorted medium and dark prints for blocks

3½ yards of light shirting print for blocks, border corner squares, and binding*

⅝ yard of dark print for border

4 yards of fabric for backing

70" × 83" piece of batting

45° kaleidoscope ruler or template plastic

Permanent marker for template plastic and fabric marker

*\*Feel free to use an assortment of scrappy shirtings to enhance the vintage effect.*

## Cutting

*All measurements include ¼"-wide seam allowances.*

**From *each* of the 46 assorted medium and dark prints, cut:**

1 strip, 6½" × 21"

**From the light shirting print, cut:**

15 strips, 6½" × 42"

4 squares, 2½" × 2½"

7 strips, 2½" × 42"

**From the dark print for border, cut:**

7 strips, 2½" × 42"

## Making the Triangle Units

If you're not using a 45° kaleidoscope ruler, first make a plastic template using the triangle pattern on page 166. Lay the template plastic on the pattern and trace the solid lines of the pattern onto the plastic. Cut out the template using a rotary cutter or scissors.

1 Place the 45° kaleidoscope ruler on a medium or dark 6½" × 21" strip so that the 6½" marking on the ruler is even with the bottom edge of the fabric. Cut four triangles from the strip, flipping the ruler after each cut. Repeat with each of the medium and dark prints. If using a template, lay the template on the medium or dark print strip, aligning the bottom of the template with the edge of the fabric. Using your rotary cutter, carefully cut along both sides of the template to cut a triangle or mark the triangles; rotate the template and cut another triangle. Repeat to cut four triangles per strip.

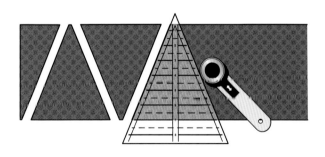

2  In the same manner, cut triangles from the light shirting 6½"-wide strips. You should get 12 triangles from each strip.

3  Place a light triangle right side down on a print triangle, offsetting the corners so they intersect at the point of the ¼" seam allowance as shown. Stitch and then press the seam allowances toward the print triangle. Repeat to make 169 pairs of triangles. The remaining muslin and print triangles will be used individually.

 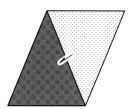

## Assembling the Quilt Top

Press the seam allowances as indicated by the arrows, or as otherwise instructed.

1  Referring to the quilt assembly diagram on page 165, arrange the triangle pairs randomly in horizontal rows with 13 units in each row. Begin row 1 and all odd-numbered rows with a print triangle. Add an individual print triangle to the end of these rows to complete the rows. Begin row 2 and all even-numbered rows with a light triangle; add an individual light triangle to the end of these rows to complete the rows. When you're pleased with the arrangement, sew the units together into rows.

Row 1

Row 2

2  Join the rows using a ½" seam allowance, alternating the odd- and even-numbered rows.

3  Trim the side edges of the quilt top by placing a long ruler along the edge of the quilt, leaving a ¼" seam allowance beyond the points of the triangles. Trim with a rotary cutter.

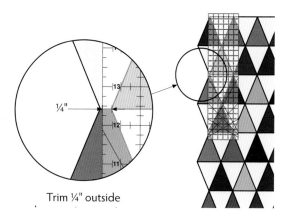

Trim ¼" outside

4  Sew two of the dark 2½" × 42" strips together end to end. Repeat to make a second strip. Measure the length of the quilt top through the center, and trim the two pieced strips to this measurement. Sew the strips to the sides of the quilt top. Crosscut one of the remaining dark 2½" × 42" strips into halves and sew one half to the short end of each remaining dark strip. Measure the width of the quilt top through the center, not including the side borders, and trim the two strips to this measurement. Sew a light 2½" square to each end of both strips, pressing the seam allowances toward the strips. Sew the border strips to the top and bottom of the quilt top.

# Finishing the Quilt

Refer to "Finishing Techniques" on page 236 for details on the following steps.

1 Layer and baste your quilt, and quilt as desired.

2 Using the light 2½"-wide strips, prepare and attach the binding.

### RE-CREATING THE PAST
Julie Hendricksen loves using cotton batting when reproducing a vintage quilt because it feels true to the spirit of the original. Plus, when you wash the new quilt, the batting will shrink just a bit to help create the slightly crinkled look of an antique.

Quilt assembly

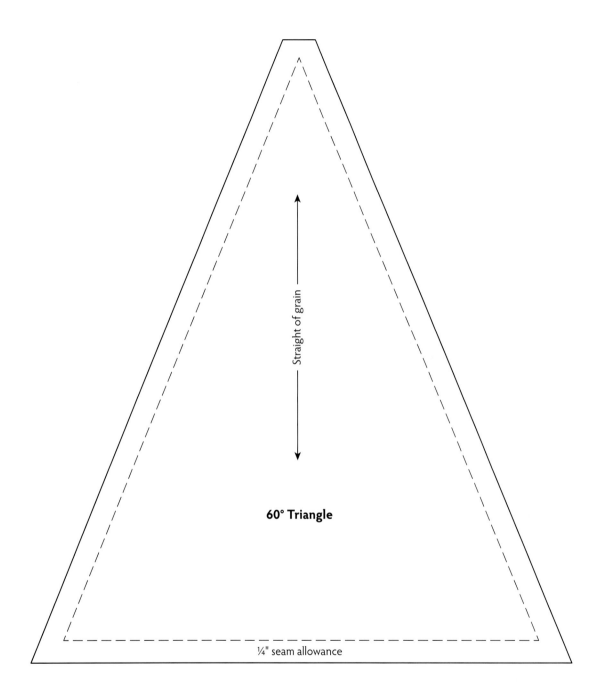

Straight of grain

**60° Triangle**

¼" seam allowance

# Love to Mary

**FINISHED QUILT:** 59" × 76" • **FINISHED BLOCK:** 6" × 6"

*Designed by Lynn Roddy Brown; pieced by Lynn Roddy Brown, Janice Thompson, and the Piecemakers of Bellaire United Methodist Church; quilted by Mary Tomlinson*

*Made as a farewell gift for a quilting-group member who was moving away, this design is easy to piece and has ample room for signatures in the block centers. The names show up nicely on a light fabric that contrasts well with the medium and dark prints.*

## Materials

*Yardage is based on 42"-wide fabric.*

20 strips, 5½" × 20", of assorted medium to dark prints for blocks

⅞ yard of cream print for blocks

1 yard of gold print for setting triangles

⅝ yard of red print for inner border

2 yards of brown print for outer border

⅔ yard of light brown print for binding

5⅛ yards of fabric for backing

67" × 84" piece of batting

Plastic-coated freezer paper

Fine-point Pigma pen in brown or black

## Cutting

*All measurements include ¼"-wide seam allowances.*

**From the cream print, cut:**
10 strips, 2½" × 42"; crosscut into 20 strips, 2½" × 20"

**From the gold print, cut:**
2 strips, 11" × 42"; crosscut into 5 squares, 11" × 11".
  Cut the squares into quarters diagonally to yield 20
  triangles.
2 squares, 6½" × 6½"; cut the squares in half
  diagonally to yield 4 triangles

**From the red print, cut:**
7 strips, 2½" × 42"

**From the brown print, cut on the *lengthwise* grain:**
4 strips, 6½" × 68"

**From the light brown print, cut:**
7 strips, 2½" × 42"

## Making the Blocks

Press the seam allowances as indicated by the arrows, or as otherwise instructed.

Blocks are made in sets of three. For each set of blocks, you'll need:

- 1 medium or dark strip, 5½" × 20"
- 1 cream strip, 2½" × 20"

1 Cut the medium or dark strip into two strips, 2½" × 20", as shown.

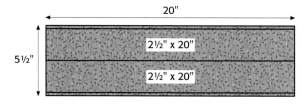

2 Sew the medium or dark strips to opposite sides of the cream strip. Press the seam allowances toward the darker strips. Trim and square up the left edge; cut three segments, 6½" wide, for blocks.

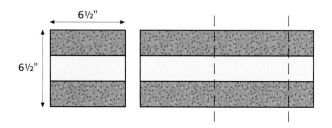

3 Repeat steps 1 and 2 to make 60 blocks.

## Assembling the Quilt Top

1 Referring to the quilt diagram below, arrange the blocks and setting triangles in diagonal rows. Be sure to scatter the identical blocks across the surface of the quilt. You'll have one extra block.

2 Sew the blocks and side setting triangles together into rows; press. Sew the rows together and press the seam allowances open. Add the corner triangles last and press the seam allowances toward the triangles.

Quilt diagram

3 Trim the edges of the quilt top, leaving a ¼" seam allowance past the points of the blocks.

4 Sew two red 2½" × 42" strips together end to end. Repeat to make a second strip. Press the seam allowances open. Measure the length of the quilt top through the center, and cut two strips to this measurement. Sew the strips to the sides of the quilt top. Press the seam allowances toward the borders. Crosscut one of the red 2½" × 42" strips into halves and sew one half to the short end of each remaining full-length red strip. Press the seam allowances open. Measure the width of the quilt top through the center, including the borders just added, and cut two strips to this measurement. Sew the strips to the top and bottom of the quilt top to complete the inner border. Press the seam allowances toward the borders.

5 Repeat to measure, stitch, and press the brown 6½" × 68" strips for the outer border.

Adding borders

## Finishing the Quilt

Refer to "Finishing Techniques" on page 236 for details on the following steps.

1 Layer and baste your quilt, and quilt as desired.

2 Using the light brown 2½"-wide strips, prepare and attach the binding.

# Grandfather Mountain

**FINISHED QUILT:** 25" × 30⅝" • **FINISHED BLOCK:** 4" × 4"

*Designed and pieced by Carol Hopkins; quilted by Lisa Ramsey*

*Civil War history is filled with intriguing characters, not all of them honorable—such as Malinda and S. M. Blalock, the bushwhacking "Bonnie and Clyde" of the North Carolina mountains. Bold peaks figure prominently in this design, but a quaint inner-border stripe softens the effect.*

## Materials

*Yardage is based on 42"-wide fabric.*

18 scraps, at least 5" × 5" each, of assorted light prints for blocks

18 scraps, at least 5" × 5" each, of assorted brown prints for blocks

18 scraps, at least 3" × 5" each, of assorted pink prints for blocks

18 scraps, at least 6" × 6" each, of assorted blue prints for blocks

¼ yard of tan print for setting triangles

1 yard of pink-and-brown stripe OR ¼ yard of nondirectional print for inner border

⅔ yard of blue print for outer border and binding

1⅛ yards of fabric for backing

33" × 39" piece of batting

### STRIPE APPEAL
Look for interesting segments within wide-striped fabrics to use as inner borders on your quilts. Fussy cut selected portions of the stripe so that all the borders are identical, and center the design on all sides of the quilt. Stripes like this often result in a clever corner effect without mitering.

## Cutting

*All measurements include ¼"-wide seam allowances.*

**From *each* of the 18 light scraps, cut:**
3 squares, 1⅞" × 1⅞"; cut in half to yield 6 triangles (108 total)

**From *each* of the 18 brown scraps, cut:**
3 squares, 1⅞" × 1⅞"; cut the squares in half diagonally to yield 6 triangles (108 total)

**From *each* of the 18 pink scraps, cut:**
2 squares, 1⅞" × 1⅞"; cut the squares in half diagonally to yield 4 triangles (72 total)

**From *each* of the 18 blue scraps, cut:**
1 square, 4⅞" × 4⅞"; cut the square in half diagonally to yield 2 triangles (36 total; 18 are extra)

**From the tan print, cut:**
1 strip, 7" × 42"; cut into:
- 3 squares, 7" × 7"; cut the squares into quarters diagonally to yield 12 triangles (2 are extra)
- 2 squares, 3¾" × 3¾"; cut the squares in half diagonally to yield 4 triangles

**From the pink-and-brown stripe, cut on the *lengthwise* grain:***
4 strips, 1¾" × 36"

**From the blue print for border and binding, cut:**
4 strips, 3" × 42"
4 strips, 2" × 42"

*\*If you're using a nondirectional print, cut the strips across the fabric width.*

## Making the Blocks

For each block, choose one pink, one brown, one blue, and one light print. Instructions are for making one block. Press the seam allowances as indicated by the arrows, or as otherwise instructed.

1 Sew a brown triangle to a light triangle to make a half-square-triangle unit. Make six matching units measuring 1½" square, including seam allowances.

Make 6.

2 Arrange the half-square-triangle units and four matching pink triangles as shown. Sew the pieces together into rows, and then join the rows.

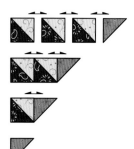 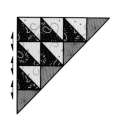

3 Sew the unit from step 2 to a blue triangle to make a block measuring 4½" square, including seam allowances. Make 18 blocks.

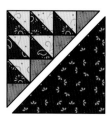 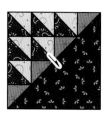

Make 18.

## Assembling the Quilt Top

1 Arrange the blocks and setting triangles in diagonal rows as shown in the assembly diagram below.

2 Sew the pieces together into rows; press. Sew the rows together and press the seam allowances open after adding each row. Add the corner triangles last; press.

Quilt assembly

3 Trim the quilt top, leaving a ¼" seam allowance beyond the points of the blocks.

4 Measure the length of the quilt top through the center and add 5". Trim two pink-and-brown strips to this measurement. Pin the strips to the sides of the quilt top, right sides together and matching the centers. Sew these strips in place, starting and stopping ¼" from the quilt corners.

Measure the quilt width, without the borders just added, and add 5". Trim the two remaining pink-and-brown strips to this measurement. Center and pin these strips to the top and bottom of the quilt top, right sides together. Sew these strips in place, starting and stopping ¼" from the quilt corners. Miter the borders at each corner of the quilt. (Visit ShopMartingale.com/HowtoQuilt if you would like illustrated instructions about mitered borders.)

5 Measure the length of the quilt top through the center and trim two of the blue 3"-wide strips to this measurement. Sew the strips to the sides of the quilt top. Measure the width of the quilt top through the center, including the borders just added, and trim the remaining blue 3"-wide strips to this measurement. Sew the strips to the top and bottom of the quilt top.

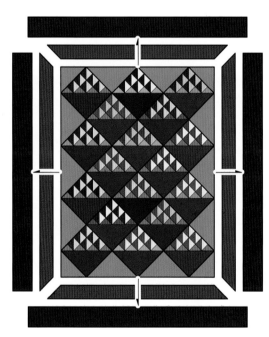

Adding borders

## Finishing the Quilt

Refer to "Finishing Techniques" on page 236 for details on the following steps.

1 Layer and baste your quilt, and quilt as desired.

2 Using the blue 2"-wide strips, prepare and attach the binding.

### OPTIONAL BUTTED-CORNER BORDER

If you've chosen a nondirectional inner-border print, you may prefer not to miter the quilt border. Follow these instructions instead.

1. Measure the length of the quilt top through the center and trim two strips to this measurement. Sew the strips to the sides of the quilt top and press the seam allowances toward the border.

2. Measure the width of the quilt top through the center, including the borders just added, and trim the two remaining strips to this measurement. Sew the strips to the top and bottom of the quilt top and press the seam allowances toward the border.

# Indigo Stars Doll Quilt

**FINISHED QUILT:** 12½" × 12½" • **FINISHED BLOCK:** 4" × 4"

*Designed and made by Jo Morton*

*Inspired by an indigo-and-muslin antique, this doll quilt's unexpected green-print binding matches the original. Jo Morton loves to tuck little quilts in out-of-the-way places, such as the bottom of a sewing basket, where they're sure to bring a smile of surprise.*

## Materials

*Yardage is based on 42"-wide fabric. Fat quarters are 18" × 21".*
4 fat quarters of indigo prints for blocks
3 fat quarters of tan-and-blue OR beige-and-blue prints for blocks
1 fat quarter of green print for binding
1 fat quarter of fabric for backing
17" × 17" piece of batting

## Cutting

*All measurements include ¼"-wide seam allowances.*

### STAR BLOCKS WITH LIGHT BACKGROUNDS
*Cutting is for 1 block. You'll need 5 total.*

**From the indigo prints, cut:**
4 squares, 1⅞" × 1⅞" (20 total)

**From the tan-and-blue or beige-and-blue prints, cut:**
4 squares, 1½" × 1½" (20 total)
1 square, 2½" × 2½" (5 total)
1 square, 3¼" × 3¼" (5 total)

### STAR BLOCKS WITH DARK BACKGROUNDS
*Cutting is for 1 block. You'll need 4 total.*

**From the indigo prints, cut:**
4 squares, 1½" × 1½" (16 total)
1 square, 2½" × 2½" (4 total)
1 square, 3¼" × 3¼" (4 total)

**From the tan-and-blue or beige-and-blue prints, cut:**
4 squares, 1⅞" × 1⅞" (16 total)

### BINDING
**From the green print, cut:**
4 strips, 1⅛" × 21"

### MAKING THE BLOCKS
Press the seam allowances as indicated by the arrows, or as otherwise instructed.

1 Draw a diagonal line from corner to corner on the wrong side of the indigo 1⅞" squares and the tan-and-blue or beige-and-blue 1⅞" squares.

2 Align two marked indigo squares on opposite corners of the tan-and-blue or beige-and-blue 3¼" square, right sides together. Note that the squares will overlap in the center. Sew a scant ¼" from each side of the drawn lines.

3 Cut the unit apart on the drawn lines and press.

4 Align one indigo 1⅞" square on the corner of the large tan-and-blue or beige-and-blue triangle. Make sure the drawn diagonal line starts at the corner and ends at the center. Sew a scant ¼" from each side of the line. Cut the unit apart on the drawn line. Press the seam allowances toward the small triangles to make a flying-geese unit. Repeat with remaining pieces to make a total of four matching flying-geese units. Trim the units to measure 1½" × 2½", including seam allowances.

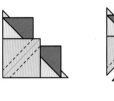

5 Lay out four tan-and-blue or beige-and-blue 1½" squares, one tan-and-blue or beige-and-blue 2½" square, and the flying-geese units in three rows. Sew the squares and units in each row together.

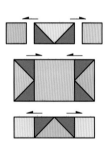

6 Pin and sew the rows together, matching seam intersections, to make a Sawtooth Star block with a light background. Press the seam allowances toward the middle row.

7 Repeat steps 2–6 to make a total of five Sawtooth Star blocks with a light background.

8 Repeat steps 2–6 using the marked tan-and-blue or beige-and-blue 1⅞" squares and remaining indigo squares to make a total of four Sawtooth Star blocks with dark backgrounds. Press the seam allowances toward the top and bottom rows (which will help you nest the seam allowances of the alternating light and dark blocks when you assemble the quilt top).

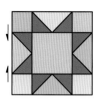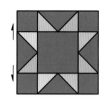

Make 5.          Make 4.

9 To reduce bulk at the seam intersections in each block, clip up to the seamline through both layers of the seam allowance, ¼" from each side of the seam intersection. (The clips will be about ½" apart.) Press the seam allowances of the flying-geese units toward the center, press the seam allowances of the squares toward the corners, and press the seam intersections open. Each Sawtooth Star block should measure 4½" square, including seam allowances. Trim as needed.

## Assembling the Quilt Top

1 Arrange the Sawtooth Star blocks in three rows of three blocks each, alternating light and dark backgrounds.

2 Sew the blocks together into rows, and then join the rows, matching the seam intersections

## Finishing the Quilt

Refer to "Finishing Techniques" on page 236 for details on the following steps.

1 Layer and baste your quilt, and quilt as desired.

2 Using the green 1⅛" wide strips and referring to "Single-Fold Binding" on page 239, prepare and attach the binding.

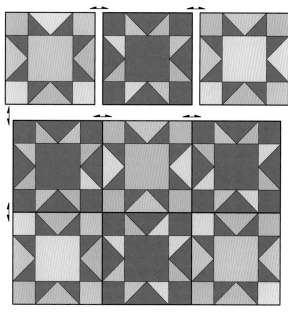

Quilt assembly

# The Bars Quilt

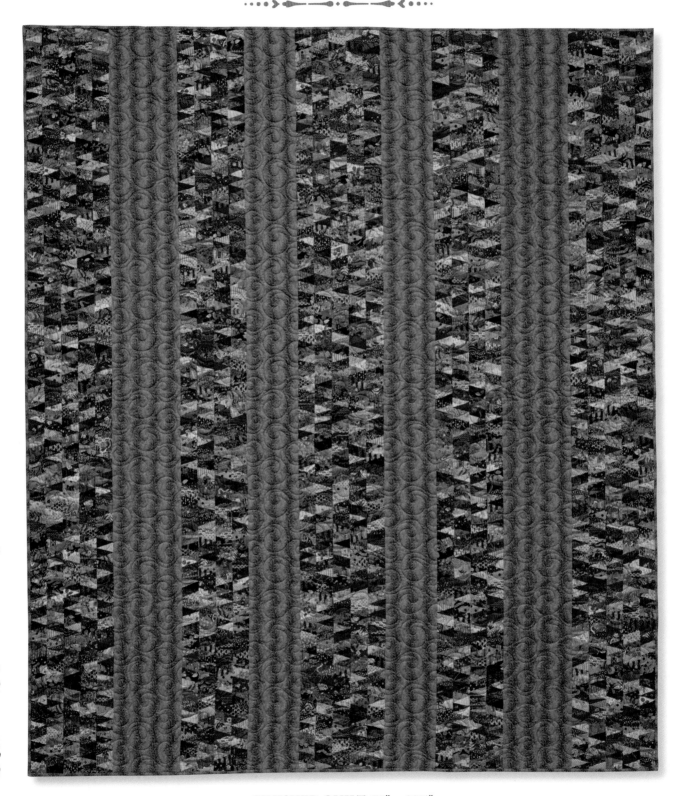

**FINISHED QUILT:** 75" × 80½"

*Designed and pieced by Biz Storms; quilted by Sandra Reed;*
*machine-quilting design by Hermione Agee*

*If you're looking for a quilt design that gives you complete freedom in choosing fabrics, allows you to make midcourse changes for width and even length, and is marvelously simple to construct, this project is for you—especially if you love small triangles.*

## Materials

*Yardage is based on 42"-wide fabric.*

10 yards *total* of assorted prints for triangles*

2½ yards of striped, directional, or large-scale print for plain bars and binding

8 yards of fabric for backing

81" × 87" piece of batting

Cardboard, fine-grain sandpaper, or template plastic

Qtools Cutting Edge Strips or masking tape (optional)

*\*Choose prints that work well with the fabric you've chosen for the plain bars. The quilt shown uses assorted prints in reds, golds, and browns, with some blues.*

## Cutting

*All measurements include ¼"-wide seam allowances.*

**From the assorted prints for triangles, cut a *total* of:**
120 strips, 2½" × 42"

**From the fabric for plain bars and binding, cut on the *lengthwise* grain:**
2 strips, 8½" × 81"
2 strips, 6¾" × 81"
4 strips, 1¾" × 81"

### SPREAD OUT THE WORK
You can always stagger the cutting over several sessions, but attempt to cut from a good cross section of colors and fabric patterns with each cutting session. Drop the cut triangles into a see-through container with a lid and gently mix them up for random color placement when it's time to sew.

## Cutting the Triangles

This quilt consists of long strips of pieced triangles stitched together to form five distinct pieced bars alternated with plain strips of fabric. To speed up the cutting of these adorable triangles, try this rotary-cutting method.

1 With raw edges aligned, stack several layers of assorted 2½"-wide strips. The strips can be flat so that you're cutting one layer of each strip, or they can be folded in half crosswise, depending on your preferences. It doesn't matter if the strips are layered with the right side facing up or down.

2 Using cardboard, fine-grain sandpaper, or template plastic and the triangle pattern on page 181, make a template. Trim the selvages from the stack of strips. Use the triangle template and a ruler to rotary cut triangle shapes from the stacked strips, flipping the template between each cut as shown.

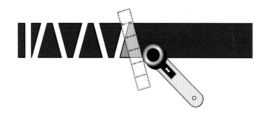

Alternatively, you can use Qtools Cutting Edge Strips or masking tape to replicate the triangle shape on a rotary-cutting ruler as shown on page 180. Cut triangle shapes, flipping the

ruler over between each cut and aligning the top and bottom edges of the triangle with the raw edges of the strips.

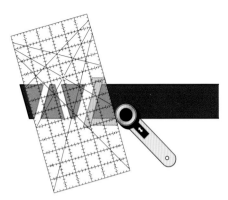

3 Continue stacking and cutting strips until you have 3500 triangles. You'll have extra triangles; these might come in handy if you want more of one color than another.

## Assembling the Bars

Once you've cut at least half of the triangles, you can begin stitching them together into the long strips.

1 With right sides together, line up the edges of two triangles, positioning them as shown. Pay careful attention to make sure the little tips of the triangles are protruding; that way the triangles will make a straight strip. Chain piece a total of five pairs of triangles. Stitch onto a scrap of fabric and stop sewing.

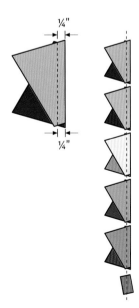

2 Cut the pairs of triangles apart for easier handling, and then stitch on the next triangle in the alternating direction as shown. Chain piece five triangles and end on a scrap of fabric.

3 Continue adding triangles in the same manner. Be sure to check the placement of each successive triangle to verify that you're maintaining a straight line along the edges of the strips and that there's a ¼" seam allowance beyond the seam intersections.

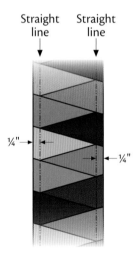

4 Continue piecing the triangle strips until you have 150 triangles in a strip. Carefully press the seam allowances in one direction, keeping the edges of the strip straight. The strip should measure approximately 84" long. Add more triangles if necessary.

5 Repeat steps 1–4 to make a total of 23 pieced triangle strips.

6 Lay out the number of triangle strips for each pieced bar, with the seam allowances in opposing directions from one strip to the next. When you are pleased with the arrangement, pin and stitch the triangle strips together. Make three triangle bars with five triangle strips in each bar. Make two triangle bars with four triangle strips in each bar.

Make 3.

Make 2.

7 Trim each triangle bar to measure 81" long and stay stitch across the ends.

## Assembling the Quilt Top

1 Lay out the triangle bars and plain bars in vertical rows, alternating them as shown.

2 Pin the bars together at each end and along the length, and then sew the bars together.

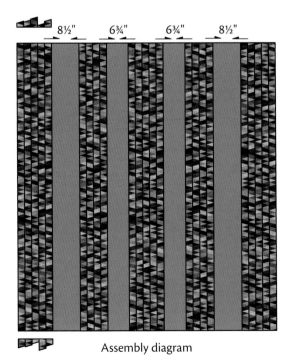

Assembly diagram

## Finishing the Quilt

Refer to "Finishing Techniques" on page 236 for details on the following steps.

1 Layer and baste your quilt, and quilt as desired.

2 Using the 1¾"-wide binding strips and referring to "Single-Fold Binding" on page 239, prepare and attach the binding.

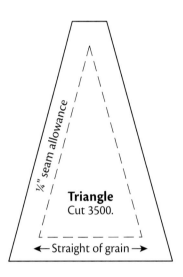

¼" seam allowance

**Triangle**
Cut 3500.

← Straight of grain →

# Remembering Chancellorsville

**FINISHED QUILT:** 73" × 93" • **FINISHED BLOCK:** 9" × 9"

*Designed and pieced by Abbi Barden; quilted by Cathy Reitan*

*This quilt honors the organizations that work so diligently to preserve Civil War battlefield sites for the education and enjoyment of us all, and for future generations. Each of the six block designs is named for a battlefield, as is the quilt itself.*

## Materials

*Yardage is based on 42"-wide fabric. Fat quarters are 18" × 21".*

12 fat quarters of assorted prints for blocks
6 fat quarters of assorted blue prints for blocks and
   inner border
4 fat quarters of assorted red prints for blocks and
   vertical sashing
2 yards of cream print for setting triangles
2¼ yards of dark print for outer border and binding
5½ yards of fabric for backing
79" × 99" piece of batting

## Cutting

*All measurements include ¼"-wide seam allowances. For scrappy blocks, use different combinations of fat quarters for the blocks in each horizontal row. Try combining medium fabrics, medium-dark fabrics, and dark fabrics for value contrast, as well as mixing different colors.*

### GETTYSBURG BLOCKS
*Cutting is for 1 block. You'll need 4 total.*

**From the first fat quarter, cut:**
2 squares, 5⅜" × 5⅜"; cut the squares in half
   diagonally to yield 4 triangles

**From the second fat quarter, cut:**
1 square, 4¼" × 4¼"; cut the square into quarters
   diagonally to yield 4 triangles
2 squares, 2⅜" × 2⅜"; cut the squares in half
   diagonally to yield 4 triangles

**From the third fat quarter, cut:**
4 rectangles, 2" × 3½"

**From the fourth fat quarter, cut:**
1 square, 3½" × 3½"

### CHICKAMAUGA BLOCKS
*Cutting is for 1 block. You'll need 4 total.*

**From the first fat quarter, cut:**
3 squares, 3⅞" × 3⅞"
3 squares, 3½" × 3½"

**From the second fat quarter, cut:**
3 squares, 3⅞" × 3⅞"

### VICKSBURG BLOCKS
*Cutting is for 1 block. You'll need 4 total.*

**From the first fat quarter, cut:**
5 squares, 3½" × 3½"

**From the second fat quarter, cut:**
4 squares, 3½" × 3½"

### MANASSAS BLOCKS
*Cutting is for 1 block. You'll need 4 total.*

**From the first fat quarter, cut:**
1 square, 7¼" × 7¼"; cut the square into quarters
   diagonally to yield 4 triangles

**From the second fat quarter, cut:**
4 rectangles, 2⅝" × 5⅝"

**From the third fat quarter, cut:**
1 square, 2⅝" × 2⅝"

### FRANKLIN BLOCKS
*Cutting is for 1 block. You'll need 4 total.*

**From the first fat quarter, cut:**
2 squares, 3⅞" × 3⅞"
4 squares, 3½" × 3½"

**From the second fat quarter, cut:**
2 squares, 3⅞" × 3⅞"
1 square, 3½" × 3½"

*(Continued on page 184)*

*(Continued from page 183)*

## THE WILDERNESS BLOCKS
*Cutting is for 1 block. You'll need 4 total.*

**From the first fat quarter, cut:**
4 squares, 3½" × 3½"

**From the second fat quarter, cut:**
2 squares, 4⅜" × 4⅜"

**From the third fat quarter, cut:**
2 squares, 4⅜" × 4⅜"
1 square, 3½" × 3½"

## SASHING, BORDERS, AND BINDING
**From the 4 red fat quarters, cut a *total* of:**
12 assorted strips, 2½" × 21"

**From the 6 blue fat quarters, cut a *total* of:**
14 assorted strips, 2½" × 21"

**From the cream print, cut:**
10 squares, 14" × 14"; cut the squares into quarters
   diagonally to yield 40 triangles
8 squares, 7¼" × 7¼"; cut the squares in half
   diagonally to yield 16 triangles

**From the dark print, cut:**
8 strips, 6½" × 42"
9 strips, 2½" × 42"

# Making the Blocks
Press the seam allowances as indicated by the arrows, or as otherwise instructed.

## GETTYSBURG BLOCKS
1 Sew 2" × 3½" rectangles to opposite sides of a 3½" square. Add 4¼" triangles to the opposite sides of the rectangles.

  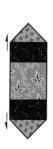

Make 1.

2 Add a 2⅜" triangle to each short edge of a 2" × 3½" rectangle. Add a 4¼" triangle to the left edge of the unit. Make two.

Make 2.

3 Join the vertical rows.

4 Sew 5⅜" triangles to opposite sides of the unit. Repeat with the remaining large triangles on the remaining sides of the unit. Make four blocks.

Make 4.

## CHICKAMAUGA BLOCKS

1 Draw a diagonal line from corner to corner on the wrong side of three matching 3⅞" squares. Place a marked square on a contrasting 3⅞" square, right sides together and raw edges aligned. Sew ¼" from both sides of the drawn line. Cut the squares apart on the line and press the seam allowances toward the darker fabric. Make six half-square-triangle units.

Make 6.

2 Lay out the half-square-triangle units and the 3½" squares in three rows as shown. Sew the pieces together into rows, and then join the rows. Make four blocks.

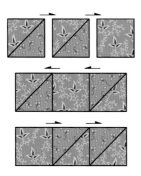
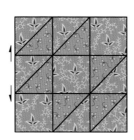

Make 4.

## VICKSBURG BLOCKS

Lay out the contrasting 3½" squares into three rows as shown. Sew the squares together into rows, and then join the rows. Make four blocks.

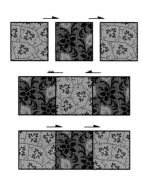
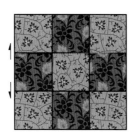

Make 4.

## MANASSAS BLOCKS

1 Lay out the triangles, rectangles, and center square as shown. (The rectangles will extend beyond the corners; you'll trim them once the block is sewn.)

2 Sew the pieces together in diagonal rows; press. Join the rows and press the seam allowances away from the center row.

3 Using a rotary ruler and cutter, trim the rectangles to square up the block corners. Make four blocks.

Make 4.

## FRANKLIN BLOCKS

1 Draw a diagonal line from corner to corner on the wrong side of two matching 3⅞" squares. Place a marked square on a contrasting 3⅞" square, right sides together and raw edges aligned. Sew ¼" from both sides of the drawn line. Cut the squares apart on the line and press the seam allowances toward the darker fabric. Make four half-square-triangle units.

2 Lay out the half-square-triangle units and the 3½" squares in three rows as shown. Sew the pieces together into rows, and then join the rows. Make four blocks.

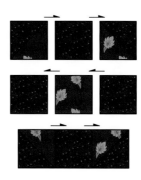
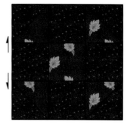

Make 4.

## THE WILDERNESS BLOCKS

1 Pin two contrasting 4⅜" squares right sides together. Draw a line diagonally from corner to corner on the lighter square. Stitch ¼" from both sides of the line. Cut the squares on the unmarked corner-to-corner diagonal, and then cut on the marked line to create four units. Press the seam allowances toward the darker fabric.

2 Pair two units as shown and stitch together on the diagonal edges. Press and trim the unit to 3½" square, including seam allowances. Repeat with the two remaining 4⅜" squares for a total of four units.

Make 4.

3 Lay out the four units from step 2 and the 3½" squares in three rows as shown. Sew the pieces together into rows, and then join the rows. Make four blocks.

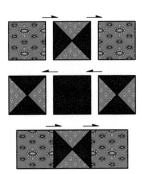 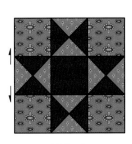

Make 4.

## Assembling the Quilt Top

1 Arrange the blocks and the cream 14" setting triangles as shown. Sew the blocks and triangles together in diagonal rows. Add the cream 7¼" corner triangles to the top and bottom of each row. Make four rows.

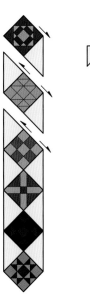

Make 4.

2 Sew the red 2½"-wide strips together end to end. Measure each row of assembled blocks from top to bottom through the center. Using the average of the four measurements, cut three sashing

strips from the red strip. Join the block rows and sashing strips, easing to fit as needed.

Quilt assembly

4 Repeat to add the dark 6½"-wide strips for the outer border.

Adding borders

3 Sew the blue 2½"-wide strips together end to end. Measure the length of the quilt top through the center, and cut two strips to this measurement. Sew the strips to the sides of the quilt top. Measure the width of the quilt top through the center, including the borders just added. Cut two strips to this measurement and sew them to the top and bottom of the quilt top to complete the inner border. (Note that in the quilt shown on page 182, the order is reversed and the top and bottom strips are added first.)

## Finishing the Quilt

Refer to "Finishing Techniques" on page 236 for details on the following steps.

1 Layer and baste your quilt, and quilt as desired.

2 Using the dark 2½"-wide strips, prepare and attach the binding.

# Civil War Log Cabin

**FINISHED QUILT:** 50" × 66½" • **FINISHED BLOCK:** 8¼" × 8¼"

*Designed and made by Mary Etherington and Connie Tesene*

*No quilt block is more American than the humble Log Cabin. Here the blocks are arranged with the strong dark-and-light diagonal shading in a straight furrows set, a nod to all the farmers and farmhands who fought side by side on our nation's farmlands.*

## Materials

*Yardage is based on 42"-wide fabric.*
18 light prints, ⅛ yard each, for blocks
18 medium-light prints, ⅛ yard each, for blocks
18 medium-dark prints, ⅛ yard each, for blocks
18 dark prints, ⅛ yard each, for blocks
⅛ yard of red fabric for block centers
½ yard of black fabric for binding
3⅓ yards of fabric for backing
54" × 70" piece of batting

## Cutting

*All measurements include ¼"-wide seam allowances. Cutting instructions for Log Cabin blocks are provided at right and on page 190.*

**From the black fabric, cut:**
6 strips, 2¼" × 42"

## Making the Blocks

The blocks are made up of rotary-cut pieces, which are indicated by number in the charts that follow. There are two different blocks: In 24 of the blocks, the last round uses a dark strip and a light strip. In the other 24 blocks, the last round uses a medium-dark strip and a medium-light strip.

Quiltmakers Mary and Connie sewed their blocks one at a time, choosing fabric as they went, rather than chain piecing them. Note that in each block there are only four different fabrics plus the red center. Of those four different fabrics, each starts as

a strip cut 1¼" × 42". The strips are then cut to make each log. Join each log to the block in the order given, pressing the seam allowances toward the log you have just added.

### LOG CABIN BLOCK 1

This block ends with a dark log and a light log. Cutting instructions are for 1 block. Make 24.

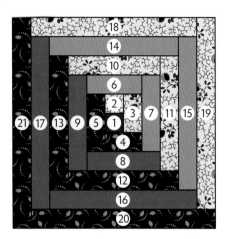

| PIECE | FABRIC | CUTTING |
|---|---|---|
| 1 | red | 1¼" × 1¼" |
| 2 | light | 1¼" × 1¼" |
| 3 | light | 1¼" × 2" |
| 4 | dark | 1¼" × 2" |
| 5 | dark | 1¼" × 2¾" |
| 6 | medium light | 1¼" × 2¾" |
| 7 | medium light | 1¼" × 3½" |
| 8 | medium dark | 1¼" × 3½" |
| 9 | medium dark | 1¼" × 4¼" |
| 10 | light | 1¼" × 4¼" |
| 11 | light | 1¼" × 5" |
| 12 | dark | 1¼" × 5" |
| 13 | dark | 1¼" × 5¾" |
| 14 | medium light | 1¼" × 5¾" |
| 15 | medium light | 1¼" × 6½" |
| 16 | medium dark | 1¼" × 6½" |
| 17 | medium dark | 1¼" × 7¼" |
| 18 | light | 1¼" × 7¼" |
| 19 | light | 1¼" × 8" |
| 20 | dark | 1¼" × 8" |
| 21 | dark | 1¼" × 8¾" |

## LOG CABIN BLOCK 2

This blocks ends with a medium-dark log and a medium-light log. Cutting instructions are for 1 block. Make 24.

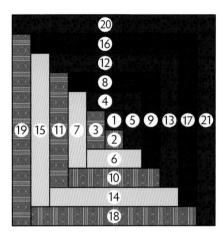

| PIECE | FABRIC | CUTTING |
|:---:|:---:|:---:|
| 1 | red | 1¼" × 1¼" |
| 2 | medium light | 1¼" × 1¼" |
| 3 | medium light | 1¼" × 2" |
| 4 | medium dark | 1¼" × 2" |
| 5 | medium dark | 1¼" × 2¾" |
| 6 | light | 1¼" × 2¾" |
| 7 | light | 1¼" × 3½" |
| 8 | dark | 1¼" × 3½" |
| 9 | dark | 1¼" × 4¼" |
| 10 | medium light | 1¼" × 4¼" |
| 11 | medium light | 1¼" × 5" |
| 12 | medium dark | 1¼" × 5" |
| 13 | medium dark | 1¼" × 5¾" |
| 14 | light | 1¼" × 5¾" |
| 15 | light | 1¼" × 6½" |
| 16 | dark | 1¼" × 6½" |
| 17 | dark | 1¼" × 7¼" |
| 18 | medium light | 1¼" × 7¼" |
| 19 | medium light | 1¼" × 8" |
| 20 | medium dark | 1¼" × 8" |
| 21 | medium dark | 1¼" × 8¾" |

## Assembling the Quilt Top

1 Arrange the blocks in eight rows of six blocks each, alternating blocks 1 and 2, and rotating the blocks to form the diagonal pattern of lights and darks.

2 Sew the blocks together into rows; press. Sew the rows together and press the seam allowances in one direction.

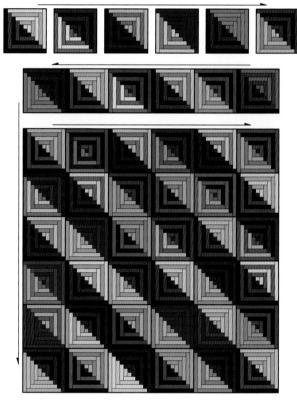

Quilt assembly

## Finishing the Quilt

Refer to "Finishing Techniques" on page 236 for details on the following steps.

1 Layer and baste your quilt, and quilt as desired.

2 Using the black 2¼"-wide strips, prepare and attach the binding.

# Vintage Patches

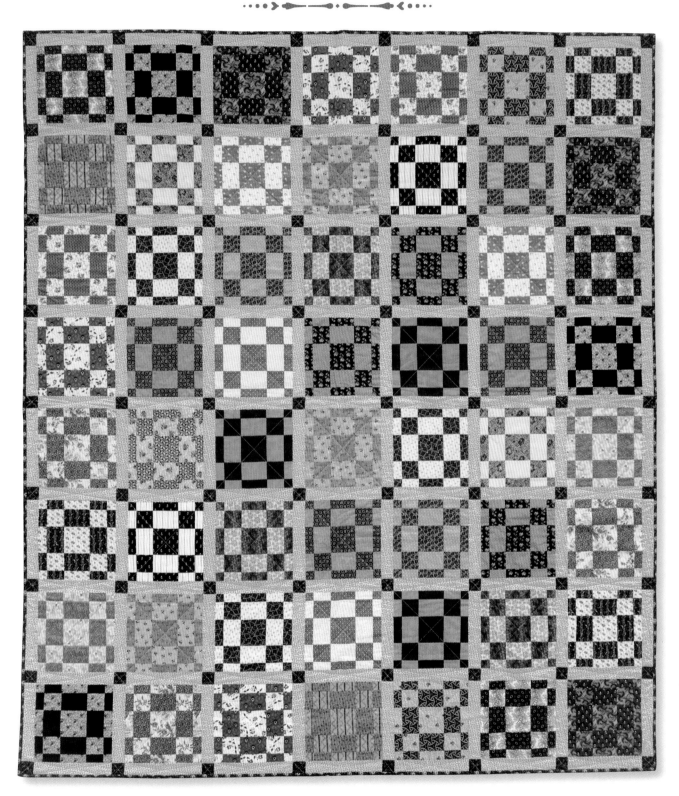

**FINISHED QUILT:** 75" × 85½" • **FINISHED BLOCK:** 9" × 9"

*Designed by Evelyn Sloppy; made by Karen Costello Soltys*

*Karen loves antiques and is very adept at making quilts that look just like those that Grandma would have made. Civil War reproduction prints are right at home here, but you could also draw from your fabric stash to create a classic scrappy quilt.*

## Materials

*Yardage is based on 42"-wide fabric. Fat quarters are 18" × 21".*

19 fat quarters OR 4 to 5 yards *total* of assorted light fabrics for blocks

19 fat quarters OR 4 to 5 yards *total* of assorted dark fabrics for blocks

2⅛ yards of light fabric for sashing

⅜ yard of dark fabric for cornerstones

¾ yard of fabric for binding

5¼ yards of fabric for backing

79" × 90" piece of batting

## Cutting

*All measurements include ¼"-wide seam allowances.*

**From *each* of the 19 light fabrics, cut:**

2 strips, 1½" × 21" (38 total)

2 strips, 2½" × 21" (38 total)

1 strip, 3½" × 21" (19 total)

**From *each* of the 19 dark fabrics, cut:**

2 strips, 1½" × 21" (38 total)

2 strips, 2½" × 21" (38 total)

1 strip, 3½" × 21" (19 total)

**From the sashing fabric, cut:**

7 strips, 9½" × 42"; crosscut into 127 pieces, 2" × 9½"

**From the cornerstone fabric, cut:**

4 strips, 2" × 42"; crosscut into 72 squares, 2" × 2"

**From the binding fabric, cut:**

9 strips, 2½" × 42"

## Making the Blocks

Press the seam allowances as indicated by the arrows, or as otherwise instructed.

1 **Block A:** Select a light and a dark fabric. You will need two 1½" × 21" strips, two 2½" × 21" strips, and one 3½" × 21" strip of each fabric. Sew into two strip sets, A and B, as shown. Crosscut strip set A into two segments, 1½" wide, and one segment, 3½" wide. Crosscut strip set B into two segments, 2½" wide.

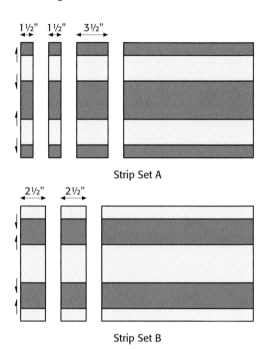

Strip Set A

Strip Set B

2 Sew the five segments together as shown to complete the block. The block should measure 9½" square, including seam allowances.

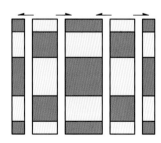

Make 30.

**3** Cut the same segments from the strip sets to make two more blocks. Each pair of strip sets will make three blocks.

**4** Repeat steps 1–3 to make 30 blocks with the other fabrics.

**5** **Block B:** Make block B in the same manner as block A, but reverse the position of lights and darks. Make 26 blocks.

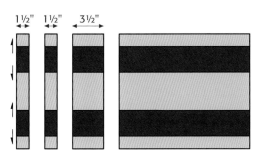

Strip Set A

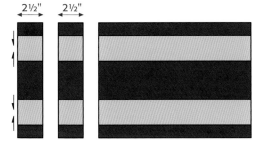

Strip Set B

Make 26.

## Assembling the Quilt Top

**1** Lay out the blocks in eight rows of seven blocks each, arranging them with the 2" × 9½" sashing strips and 2" cornerstones as shown in the quilt diagram below. Note that the B blocks are placed around the outside of the quilt top and the A blocks fill the quilt center.

**2** Sew the pieces together into rows, and then join the rows.

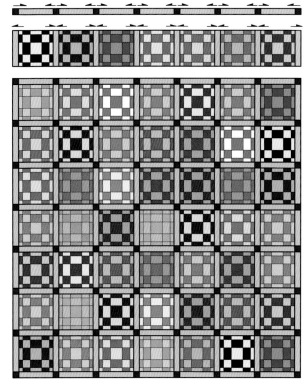

Quilt assembly

## Finishing the Quilt

Refer to "Finishing Techniques" on page 236 for details on the following steps.

**1** Layer and baste your quilt, and quilt as desired.

**2** Using the 2½"-wide binding strips, prepare and attach the binding.

# Baskets for Betsy

**FINISHED QUILT:** 23½" × 28½" • **FINISHED BLOCK:** 4" × 4"

*Designed and made by Carol Hopkins*

*If you're the type who loves to use every color the world has to offer, making this quilt will be a pure delight. The Basket blocks are straightforward and classic, while the zigzag setting triangles are eye-catchingly scrappy and just plain fun.*

## Materials

*Yardage is based on 42"-wide fabric.*

⅜ yard of light print for block backgrounds

11 scraps, at least 6" × 6" each, of assorted dark prints for blocks

52 scraps, at least 3" × 3" each, of assorted medium prints for setting triangles

½ yard of dark brown print for inner border and binding

⅜ yard of paisley print for outer border

⅞ yard of fabric for backing

30" × 35" piece of batting

### EFFECTIVE ZIGZAGS

Select prints of equal color value for the setting triangles so that your eye sees a colorful, but unbroken, zigzag between the Basket blocks. When choosing the scale of prints in the triangles, feel free to incorporate lots of variety.

## Cutting

*All measurements include ¼"-wide seam allowances.*

**From the light print, cut:**

11 squares, 2⅞" × 2⅞"; cut the squares in half diagonally to yield 22 triangles

22 squares, 1⅞" × 1⅞"; cut the squares in half diagonally to yield 44 triangles

22 rectangles, 1½" × 2½"

11 squares, 1½" × 1½"

**From *each* of the 11 dark scraps, cut:**

1 square, 2⅞" × 2⅞"; cut the square in half diagonally to yield 2 triangles (22 total; 11 are extra)

3 squares, 1⅞" × 1⅞"; cut the squares in half diagonally to yield 6 triangles (66 total)

**From *each* of the 52 medium scraps, cut:**

1 square, 2⅞" × 2⅞"; cut the square in half diagonally to yield 2 triangles (104 total)

**From the dark brown print, cut:**

4 strips, 1¾" × 42"

4 strips, 2" × 42"

**From the paisley print, cut:**

4 strips, 2½" × 42"

## Making the Blocks

The light print is paired with a different dark print in each of the Basket blocks. Instructions are for making one block; use the same dark print throughout the block. Press the seam allowances as indicated by the arrows, or as otherwise instructed.

1 Sew a light 2⅞" triangle and a dark 2⅞" triangle together to make a half-square-triangle unit measuring 2½" square, including seam allowances.

2 Sew a light 1⅞" triangle to a dark 1⅞" triangle to make a half-square-triangle unit measuring 1½" square, including seam allowances. Make four. Sew these units into two pairs, rotating the triangles so that the pairs are mirror images.

Make 1 of each.

3 Sew one of the units from step 2 to the unit from step 1, orienting the units as shown.

4 Sew a light 1½" square to the remaining unit from step 2. Sew this assembled unit to the unit from step 3.

 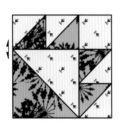

5 Sew a dark 1⅞" triangle to one end of a light 1½" × 2½" rectangle. Make two units, orienting the dark triangles as shown.

  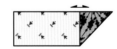

  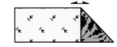

6 Sew the units from step 5 to the unit from step 4.

 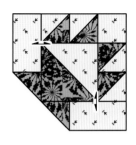

7 Sew the remaining light 2⅞" triangle to the bottom corner of the basket unit. Make 11 blocks measuring 4½" square, including seam allowances.

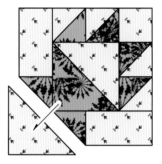

Make 11.

# Making the Setting-Triangle Units

This quilt has three different setting-triangle units, all assembled from the medium print triangles. Pay close attention to the orientation of the triangles in each unit.

### SIDE-TRIANGLE UNIT

Sew two contrasting triangles together to make a half-square-triangle unit. Orient the unit so that the seam runs from the upper-left corner to the lower-right corner. Sew one triangle to the top and one triangle to the right edge of the half-square-triangle unit as shown. Make 20.

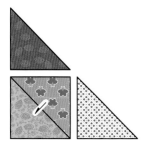 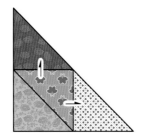

Make 20.

### TOP/BOTTOM-TRIANGLE UNIT

Follow the instructions for the side-triangle units, but orient the half-square-triangle unit so that its seam runs from the lower-left corner to the upper-right corner. Make two.

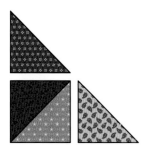 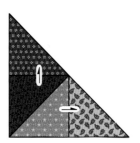

Make 2.

### CORNER-TRIANGLE UNIT

Sew two contrasting triangles together as shown. Make eight.

Make 8.

# Assembling the Quilt Top

1. Arrange the Basket blocks and setting-triangle units in three rows as shown below. Rows 1 and 3 are the same; each has four Basket blocks, six side-triangle units, and four corner-triangle units. Row 2 has three Basket blocks, eight side-triangle units, and two top/bottom-triangle units. Sew the pieces together into rows.

Rows 1 and 3.
Make 2.

Row 2.
Make 1.

2. Trim and square up the rows, leaving a ¼" seam allowance beyond the points of the blocks.

3 Sew the rows together as shown.

Quilt assembly

4 Measure the length of the quilt top through the center and trim two dark brown 1¾"-wide strips to this measurement. Sew the strips to the sides of the quilt top. Measure the width of the quilt top through the center, including the borders just added, and trim the remaining dark brown 1¾"-wide strips to this measurement. Sew the strips to the top and bottom of the quilt top to complete the inner border.

5 Repeat to add the paisley 2½"-wide strips for the outer border.

Adding borders

## Finishing the Quilt

Refer to "Finishing Techniques" on page 236 for details on the following steps.

1 Layer and baste your quilt, and quilt as desired.

2 Using the dark brown 2"-wide strips, prepare and attach the binding.

# Blue and Gray

**FINISHED QUILT:** 40¼" × 47¾"

**FINISHED BLOCKS:** 2¼" × 2¼" and 5¼" × 5¼"

*Designed and made by Mary Etherington and Connie Tesene*

*The humble Nine Patch block has been a favorite among quilters for over a century, due in part to the simplicity that makes it perfect for using up scraps. By making larger blocks, you can easily turn this small version into a bed-sized quilt.*

## Materials

*Yardage is based on 42"-wide fabric.*

15 assorted light prints, ⅛ yard each, for Nine Patch and Red Cross blocks

15 assorted dark blue prints, ⅛ yard each, for Nine Patch blocks

5 assorted red prints, ⅛ yard each, for Red Cross blocks

5 assorted medium blue and gray prints, ¼ yard each, for sashing

⅞ yard of dark blue print for sashing, cornerstones, and binding

2½ yards of fabric for backing

44" × 52" piece of batting

## Cutting

*All measurements include ¼"-wide seam allowances.*

**From the assorted light prints, cut:**
120 squares, 2¼" × 2¼"
152 squares, 1¼" × 1¼"

**From the assorted dark blue prints, cut:**
150 squares, 2¼" × 2¼"

**From the assorted red prints, cut:**
76 squares, 1¼" × 1¼"
38 rectangles, 1¼" × 2¾"

**From the assorted medium blue and gray prints, cut:**
49 rectangles, 2¾" × 5¾"

**From the dark blue print, cut:**
4 strips, 2¾" × 42"; crosscut into:
• 22 rectangles, 2¾" × 5¾"
• 4 squares, 2¾" × 2¾"
2¼"-wide bias strips to total 186"

## Making the Nine Patch Blocks

Use four matching light 2¼" squares and five matching dark 2¼" squares for each block. Press the seam allowances as indicated by the arrows, or as otherwise instructed.

1 Sew two rows using dark squares on opposite sides of a light square. Make one row with light squares on opposite sides of a dark square.

Make 2.          Make 1.

2 Sew the rows together with the dark/light/dark rows on the top and bottom to complete a Nine Patch block. The block should measure 5¾" square, including seam allowances. Make 30 blocks.

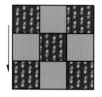

Nine Patch block.
Make 30.

## Making the Red Cross Blocks

Use four matching light 1¼" squares and a matching set of two red 1¼" squares and one red 1¼" × 2¾" rectangle for each block.

1 Sew light squares to opposite sides of a red square. Make two.

Make 2.

2 Sew the matching rows from step 1 to each long side of the red rectangle. The block should measure 2¾" square, including seam allowances. Make 38 blocks.

Red Cross block.
Make 38.

## Assembling the Quilt Top

1 Lay out five Nine Patch blocks alternating with four medium blue or gray rectangles as shown. Add a dark blue rectangle to each end of the row. Sew the blocks and sashing rectangles together. Make six block rows.

Make 6 rows.

2 Lay out five medium blue or gray rectangles alternating with six Red Cross blocks as shown. Sew the blocks and rectangles together. Make five sashing rows.

Make 5 rows.

3 Lay out five dark blue rectangles alternating with four Red Cross blocks as shown. Add a dark blue square to each end of the row. Make two for the top and bottom borders.

Make 2 borders.

4 Join the block rows, sashing rows, and top and bottom borders as shown. Press.

Quilt plan

## Finishing the Quilt

Refer to "Finishing Techniques" on page 236 for details on the following steps.

1 Layer and baste your quilt, and quilt as desired.

2 You can leave the quilt top square, or create rounded corners as shown in the photo on page 199. Simply place a 5"-diameter plate or cardboard circle on the corner block, trace the curve, and trim. Then use the dark blue 2¼"-wide bias strips to prepare and attach the binding.

# Vintage LeMoyne Stars

**FINISHED QUILT:** 60" × 77" • **FINISHED BLOCK:** 8½" × 8½"

*Designed and made by Gayle Bong*

*The classic LeMoyne Star shines beautifully in 1800s reproduction prints, but it will look great no matter what fabrics you choose. The diamonds in the stars are cut from 2¼"-wide strips, but an array of 2½" strips could always be trimmed down.*

## Materials

*Yardage is based on 42"-wide fabric.*

1⅞ yards *total* of assorted light scraps for blocks and borders

1 yard *total* of assorted medium scraps for blocks and borders

2⅛ yards *total* of assorted dark scraps for blocks and borders

⅞ yard of cream print for inner border

⅝ yard of dark print for binding

4⅛ yards of fabric for backing

64" × 80" piece of batting

## Cutting

*All measurements include ¼"-wide seam allowances.*

### LIGHT LEMOYNE STAR BLOCKS

*Cutting is for 1 block. You'll need 28 total.*

**From the assorted light scraps, cut:**
1 strip, 2¼" × 18" (28 total)

**From the assorted medium scraps, cut:**
1 strip, 2¼" × 18" (28 total)

**From the assorted dark scraps, cut:**
1 strip, 4¾" × 18" (28 total); crosscut into 1 square, 4¾" × 4¾". Cut the square into quarters diagonally to yield 4 triangles (112 total). Trim the remainder of the strip to 3" wide and cut 4 squares, 3" × 3" (112 total).

### DARK LEMOYNE STAR BLOCKS

*Cutting is for 1 block. You'll need 24 total.*

**From the assorted light scraps, cut:**
1 strip, 4¾" × 18" (24 total); crosscut into 1 square, 4¾" × 4¾". Cut the square into quarters diagonally to yield 4 triangles (96 total). Trim the remainder of the strip to 3" wide and cut 4 squares, 3" × 3" (96 total).

**From the assorted medium scraps, cut:**
1 strip, 2¼" × 18" (24 total)

**From the assorted dark scraps, cut:**
1 strip, 2¼" × 18" (24 total)

### INNER BORDER AND BINDING

**From the cream print, cut:**
4 squares, 4⅝" × 4⅝"
4 strips, 5" × 42"; crosscut into 30 squares, 5" × 5". Cut the squares in half diagonally to yield 60 triangles.

**From the assorted dark scraps, cut:**
30 squares, 3⅝" × 3⅝"; cut the squares in half diagonally to yield 60 triangles

**From the dark print for binding, cut:**
7 strips, 2¼" × 42"

## Making the Light LeMoyne Star Blocks

Press the seam allowances as indicated by the arrows, or as otherwise instructed.

1. Aligning the 45° line of a ruler with the bottom of a light 2¼" × 18" strip, trim the left end of the strip as shown. Make four more cuts at the same angle, 2¼" apart, to yield four diamonds for one block. Repeat with the remaining 2¼" × 18" strips to make a total of 112 light diamonds and 112 medium diamonds.

2 Choose four light diamonds, four medium diamonds, four dark triangles, and four dark squares. With the light diamond on top, sew each light diamond to a medium diamond. Avoid stitching into the seam allowance at the inside corners indicated by the dot in the illustration. Make four.

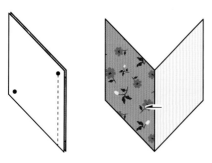

3 In the same manner, sew two pairs of diamonds together to make a half-star unit, and then sew the two half-star units together. Before pressing,

undo two stitches in the seam allowance at the center of the star. This will let the seam allowances fall open in a pinwheel fashion, helping to distribute the bulk at the center of the block. Be careful not to stretch the bias edge of the diamonds as you press.

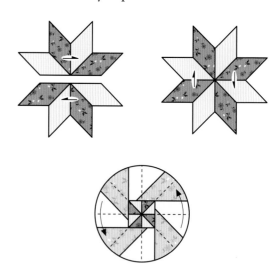

## HOW TO SEW SET-IN PIECES

The seams of typical patchwork run from raw edge to raw edge, crossing into the seam allowances at each end. There are many beautiful patterns that require set-in seams where stitching stops at an inside corner where three seams meet. It takes just a little practice on a few blocks to master them. To aid in accomplishing this, you may find it most helpful to use an open-toe presser foot, so it's easier to see exactly where you are sewing.

It helps to mark the seam intersections on the back of each patch with a dot, and then match the dots as you sew. A template to mark the seam allowances is helpful. Use a large needle to poke a hole in the template where the seams intersect. Align the edges of the template with the edges of the patch and make a mark using a pencil through the hole. An alternate method is to mark the back of each patch with an × where the seams intersect. Measure ¼" from each edge of the patch and make a mark. Even if you visualize the dot, it helps to use a pin to indicate

precisely where the seam begins or ends at the inside corner; then the seams may be sewn from either direction.

Backstitching is required where the three seams meet, because there will not be seams crossing one another to anchor the threads. Some machines seem to be a little fussy about responding to the backstitch lever, so try backstitching four to five stitches away from the intersection. That way, if any stitches do cross into the seam allowance, they can be removed without cutting backstitches.

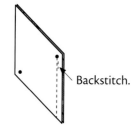
Backstitch.

4 Sew dark triangles between the star points at the sides of the block. With right sides together, match points of a medium diamond and a dark triangle as shown. Stitch the seam, clip the threads, and remove the pieces from the machine. Match the other point of the dark triangle to the light diamond and sew. Press the seam allowances of the set-in background pieces to pinwheel as described in step 3. Repeat with all four triangles.

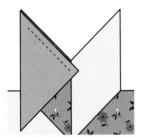 

5 Sew a dark square into each corner in the same manner. Press the seam allowances of the set-in background pieces to pinwheel as described in step 3. Repeat to make a total of 28 light LeMoyne Star blocks.

Light LeMoyne Star block.
Make 28.

## Making the Dark LeMoyne Star Blocks

Refer to the instructions in "Making the Light LeMoyne Star Blocks" on page 203 to make 24 dark LeMoyne Star blocks. You will use the medium and dark 2¼" × 18" strips to cut four medium diamonds and four dark diamonds for each block (96 total of each). Sew the diamond pairs together with the medium diamond on top. You will also use four light triangles and four light squares for each block.

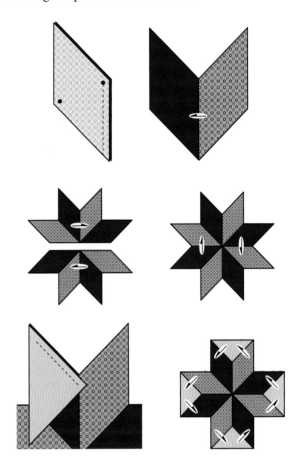

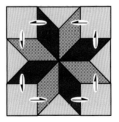

Dark LeMoyne Star block.
Make 24.

# Assembling the Quilt Top

1 Arrange the dark LeMoyne Star blocks in six rows of four blocks each. Sew the blocks together into rows, pressing the seam allowances in opposite directions from row to row. Sew the rows together and press the seam allowances in one direction.

2 Layer two cream triangles wrong sides together, and trim the top points as shown to create trapezoids 3¼" tall. Repeat with the remaining cream triangles to make 60 trapezoids.

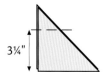 

3¼"

3 Sew a dark triangle to the angled edge of each cream trapezoid. Make 30 units with the triangle on the right side and 30 units with the triangle on the left side.

Make 30 each.

4 Join 12 trapezoid units as shown, and add a cream square to each end of the strip. Make two strips for the top and bottom borders. Join 18 trapezoid units as shown. Make two strips for the side borders.

Top/bottom border.
Make 2.

Side border.
Make 2.

5 Sew the side borders to the quilt top, positioning the dark edges of the pieced strips toward the quilt center and matching the seam of every third unit to the seams between the blocks. Ease to fit as necessary. Sew the top and bottom borders to the quilt top in the same manner.

6 Arrange the light LeMoyne Star blocks around the quilt center. Sew the seven blocks along each side together, and then stitch the strips to the quilt top. Sew the seven blocks along the top and bottom together, and then stitch the strips to the quilt top.

7 Sew a line of stay stitching ⅛" from the edges of the quilt top to prevent the seams in the blocks from coming loose.

## Finishing the Quilt

Refer to "Finishing Techniques" on page 236 for details on the following steps.

1 Layer and baste your quilt, and quilt as desired.

2 Using the 2¼"-wide binding strips, prepare and attach the binding.

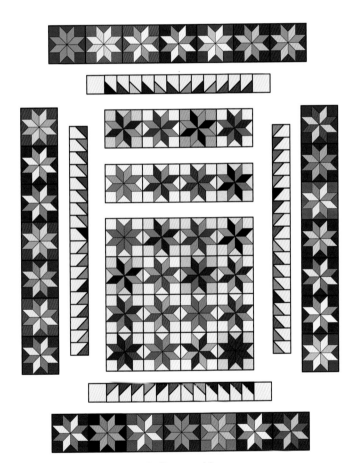

Quilt assembly

# Men at Work

**FINISHED QUILT:** 63½" × 74" • **FINISHED BLOCK:** 5¼" × 5¼"

*Designed and made by Julie Hendricksen*

*Darting Bird blocks fly in formation in diagonal bands of classic late-19th-century colors. Mix up prints within each color family for plenty of interest. (Give the blocks a half turn, and you'll see the resemblance to men-at-work icons that inspired the quilt's name!)*

## Materials

*Yardage is based on 42"-wide fabric. Fat eighths are 9" × 21".*

42 fat eighths OR ¼-yard cuts in the following amounts and print colors for blocks: 3 brown, 8 indigo, 6 burgundy, 5 navy, 5 gray, 6 red, 4 black, and 5 pink*

4 yards of muslin for blocks

⅝ yard of brown print for binding

4½ yards of fabric for backing

71" × 81" piece of batting

*Julie used an assortment of prints in each color (for example, 3 different browns), but you could use a single print for each color.*

## Cutting

*All measurements include ¼"-wide seam allowances.*

### From *each* fat eighth or ¼ yard, cut the following pieces to make 2 blocks:

4 squares, 2⅝" × 2⅝"; cut the squares in half diagonally to yield 8 triangles (336)

2 squares, 2¼" × 2¼" (84 total)

1 square, 4⅜" × 4⅜"; cut the square in half diagonally to yield 2 triangles (84 total)

### From the muslin, cut:

14 strips, 5¾" × 42"; crosscut into 84 squares, 5¾" × 5¾"

5 strips, 2¼" × 42"; crosscut into 84 squares, 2¼" × 2¼"

17 strips, 2⅝" × 42"; crosscut into 252 squares, 2⅝" × 2⅝". Cut the squares in half diagonally to yield 504 triangles.

### From the brown print for binding, cut:

7 strips, 2½" × 42"

## Making the Blocks

Press the seam allowances as indicated by the arrows, or as otherwise instructed.

1  Sew together a muslin 2⅝" triangle and a print 2⅝" triangle to make a half-square-triangle unit. Repeat to make three more half-square-triangle units using the same print. The units should measure 2¼" square, including seam allowances.

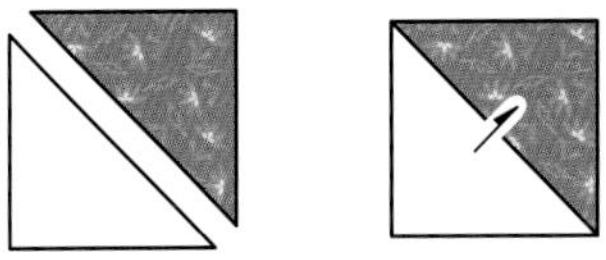

Make 4.

2  Join the half-square-triangle units in pairs, taking care to orient them correctly as shown.

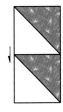

3  Sew muslin triangles to two adjacent sides of a matching-print 2¼" square. Sew the completed unit to a matching-print 4⅜" triangle. The unit should measure 4" square, including seam allowances.

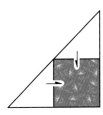
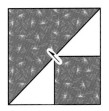

4 Sew the left unit from step 2 to the left edge of the unit from step 3 as shown.

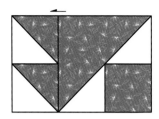

5 Sew a muslin square to the left end of the remaining half-square-triangle pair from step 2.

6 Stitch the unit from step 5 to the top edge of the unit from step 4 to complete the block.

7 Repeat to make a total of 84 blocks, 2 from each fabric. When all of the blocks are pieced, you should have the following totals: 6 brown, 16 indigo, 12 burgundy, 10 navy, 10 gray, 12 red, 8 black, and 10 pink blocks. The blocks should measure 5¾" square, including seam allowances.

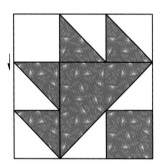

Make 84 total.

## Assembling the Quilt Top

1 Referring to the photo on page 208 and the quilt assembly diagram below, arrange the pieced blocks and muslin squares so that the colors run in diagonal rows in the following order, beginning in the upper-right corner: navy, brown, burgundy, black, pink, indigo, red, gray, navy, burgundy, indigo, and brown.

2 Sew the blocks together into rows, and then join the rows.

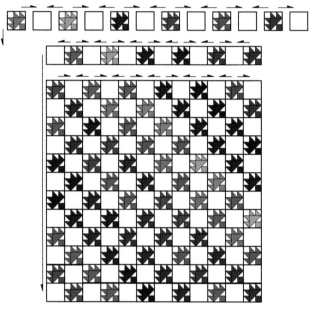

Quilt assembly

## Finishing the Quilt

Refer to "Finishing Techniques" on page 236 for details on the following steps.

1 Layer and baste your quilt, and quilt as desired.

2 Using the brown 2½"-wide strips, prepare and attach the binding.

## QUEEN-SIZE OPTION

To make a queen-size version of the Men at Work quilt that is 18 blocks wide, 18 blocks long, and finishes at 95" × 95", you'll need the following:

3 additional fat eighths OR ¾ yard of brown print
1 additional fat eighth OR ¼-yard cut of gray print
7¾ yards *total* of muslin
¾ yard *total* of brown print for binding
9 yards of fabric for backing
107" × 107" piece of batting

## Cutting

**From *each* fat eighth or ¼ yard, cut the following pieces to make 4 blocks:**
8 squares, 2⅝" × 2⅝"; cut the squares in half diagonally to yield 16 triangles
4 squares, 2¼" × 2¼"
2 squares, 4⅜" × 4⅜"; cut the squares in half diagonally to yield 4 triangles

**From the muslin, cut:**
27 strips, 5¾" × 42"; crosscut into 162 squares, 5¾" × 5¾"
10 strips, 2¼" × 42"; crosscut into 162 squares, 2¼" × 2¼"
33 strips, 2⅝" × 42"; crosscut into 486 squares, 2⅝" × 2⅝". Cut the squares in half diagonally to yield 972 triangles.

**From the brown print for binding, cut:**
9 strips, 2½" × 42"

Referring to the instructions on page 209, piece 162 blocks in the following quantities: 22 brown, 26 indigo, 22 burgundy, 20 navy, 24 gray, 24 red, 18 pink, and 10 black. Arrange the blocks and squares in 18 rows of 18 blocks each in the color order shown in the quilt assembly diagram, beginning in the upper-right corner. After placing the second row of navy blocks on the lower-left side, continue to place the remaining blocks in this order: red, gray, brown, pink, and black.

# Peony Star

**FINISHED QUILT:** 50¼" × 50¼" • **FINISHED BLOCK:** 9" × 9"

*Designed and made by Kathleen Tracy*

*This charming and unusual version of the Peony Star block blooms in vivid colors reminiscent of old-fashioned country gardens. The muted brown stripes of a reproduction print encircle the quilt center to give a subtle antique touch.*

## Materials

*Yardage is based on 42"-wide fabric. Fat eighths are 9" × 21".*

9 fat eighths of assorted light prints for block backgrounds

9 fat eighths of assorted medium prints for peonies

Scraps of assorted green prints for stems and leaves (some prints may be repeated)

⅜ yard of beige print for setting squares

½ yard of light floral for setting triangles

1⅝ yards of lengthwise brown stripe for border

⅝ yard of pink print for binding

3¼ yards of fabric for backing

58" × 58" piece of batting

Template plastic

Bias bar

## Cutting

*All measurements include ¼"-wide seam allowances.*

**From *each* of the 9 light fat eighths, cut:**
3 squares, 3⅛" × 3⅛" (27 total)
3 squares, 2¾" × 2¾" (27 total)
1 square, 5" × 5" (9 total)

**From *each* of the 9 medium fat eighths, cut:**
3 squares, 3⅛" × 3⅛" (27 total)
3 squares, 2¾" × 2¾" (27 total)

**From the assorted green prints, cut:**
9 strips, 1¼" × 8½"

**From the beige print, cut:**
4 squares, 9½" × 9½"

**From the light floral, cut:**
2 squares, 7¼" × 7¼"; cut the squares in half diagonally to yield 4 triangles
2 squares, 14" × 14"; cut the squares into quarters diagonally to yield 8 triangles

**From the brown stripe, cut on the *lengthwise* grain:**
4 strips, 6¼" × 52"

**From the pink print, cut:**
7 strips, 2½" × 42"

## Making the Blocks

For each Peony Star block, choose a medium print, a light background print, and a green print for the stems and leaves. Press the seam allowances as indicated by the arrows, or as otherwise instructed.

1. Fold a green 1¼" × 8½" strip in half, wrong sides together, and press. Sew ¼" from the raw edges to form a tube. Trim the seam allowance to ⅛".

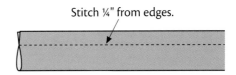

Stitch ¼" from edges.

2. Insert a bias bar into the sewn tube, turning the seam to the flat side of the bar so that it is hidden. Press the seam flat and remove the tube carefully (the bias bars can get very hot).

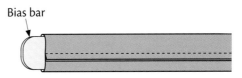

Bias bar

3. Pin the finished stem diagonally on a light 5" square.

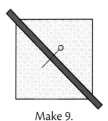

Make 9.

**4** Using the pattern on page 215, prepare 2 matching leaves (you will need 18 total) for your favorite method of appliqué. Kathleen Tracy used needle-turn appliqué to give her reproduction quilt a handmade look. Set the leaves aside.

**5** Draw a diagonal line from corner to corner on the wrong side of a light 3⅛" square. Place the marked square on a medium 3⅛" square, right sides together and raw edges aligned. Sew ¼" from the drawn line on both sides. Cut the squares apart on the line and press the seam allowances toward the medium print. Make 6 half-square-triangle units for each block (54 total).

Make 6
for each block.

**6** Sew a unit from step 5 together with a light 2¾" square. Make 3 for each block (27 total). Sew the remaining 3 units from step 5 together with matching medium 2¾" squares. Make 3 for each block (27 total).

Make 3
for each block.          Make 3
for each block.

**7** Lay out the matching units from step 6 as shown, sew, and press. Make 3 for each block (27 total).

Make 3
for each block.

**8** Sew the matching units from step 7 and the light 5" square from step 3 together into rows. Sew the rows together and press. Appliqué the stem and leaves to the block using your preferred method. Make nine blocks.

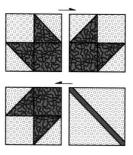 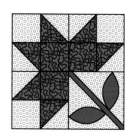

Make 9.

## Assembling the Quilt Top

**1** Lay out the blocks, beige setting squares, and floral side and corner setting triangles in diagonal rows.

**2** Sew the pieces together into rows, and then sew the rows together, matching seam intersections. Add the corner triangles last and press the seam allowances toward the triangles. Trim and square up the quilt top, leaving 1¼" beyond the points of all the blocks for seam allowances.

Quilt assembly

3 Measure the length of the quilt top through the center. Cut two of the brown 6¼" × 52" strips to this measurement and sew them to the sides of the quilt top. Measure the width of the quilt top through the center, including the borders just added. Cut the remaining brown 6¼" × 52" strips to this measurement and sew them to the top and bottom of the quilt top.

## Finishing the Quilt

Refer to "Finishing Techniques" on page 236 for details on the following steps.

1 Layer and baste your quilt, and quilt as desired.

2 Using the pink 2½"-wide strips, prepare and attach the binding.

Adding borders

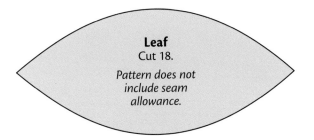

**Leaf**
Cut 18.

*Pattern does not include seam allowance.*

*Peony Star*

# Woven Stars

**FINISHED QUILT:** 16½" × 20½" • **FINISHED BLOCK:** 8" × 8"

*Designed and made by Rebecca Silbaugh*

*Stars created from scrappy, simple pieces hold a timeless appeal. This small quilt, made entirely of half-square-triangle units and solid squares, weaves those stars together in a creative way that will have you chomping at the bit to break into your stash!*

## Materials

*Yardage is based on 42"-wide fabric. Fat quarters are 18" × 21".*

24 squares, 3" × 3", of assorted light prints for blocks

12 squares, 3" × 3", of assorted medium prints for blocks

12 squares, 3" × 3", of assorted dark prints for blocks

32 squares, 2½" × 2½", of assorted light prints for blocks

¼ yard of brown stripe for binding

1 fat quarter of fabric for backing

20" × 24" piece of batting

## Cutting

*All measurements include ¼"-wide seam allowances.*

**From the brown stripe, cut:**

2 strips, 2¼" × 42"

## Making the Blocks

Press the seam allowances as indicated by the arrows, or as otherwise instructed.

1. Draw a diagonal line from corner to corner on the wrong side of each light 3" square. Place a marked square on each medium and dark 3" square, right sides together. Stitch ¼" from both sides of the marked line. Cut the squares apart on the marked line and press. Make a total of 48 half-square-triangle units and trim each unit to 2½" square, including seam allowances.

Make 24.   Make 24.

2. Arrange six dark half-square-triangle units, four medium half-square-triangle units, and six light 2½" squares into four horizontal rows of four pieces each as shown, paying careful attention to the positioning of the half-square-triangle units. Sew the pieces together into rows, and then join the rows. Repeat to make a total of four blocks.

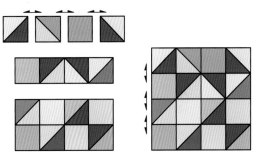

Make 4.

## Assembling the Quilt Top

1 Arrange the blocks into two horizontal rows of two blocks each, rotating the blocks as shown to create the pattern.

2 Sew the blocks together into rows, and then join the rows.

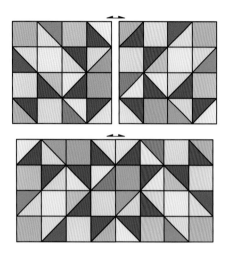

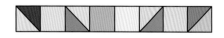

Make 2.

3 Join four medium half-square-triangle units and four light 2½" squares into a horizontal row, rotating the half-square-triangle units as shown. Press the seam allowances open. Repeat to make a total of two border strips.

4 Sew the border strips to the top and bottom of the quilt top as shown.

Quilt assembly

## Finishing the Quilt

Refer to "Finishing Techniques" on page 236 for details on the following steps.

1 Layer and baste your quilt, and quilt as desired.

2 Using the brown 2¼"-wide strips, prepare and attach the binding.

# Lake Cabin

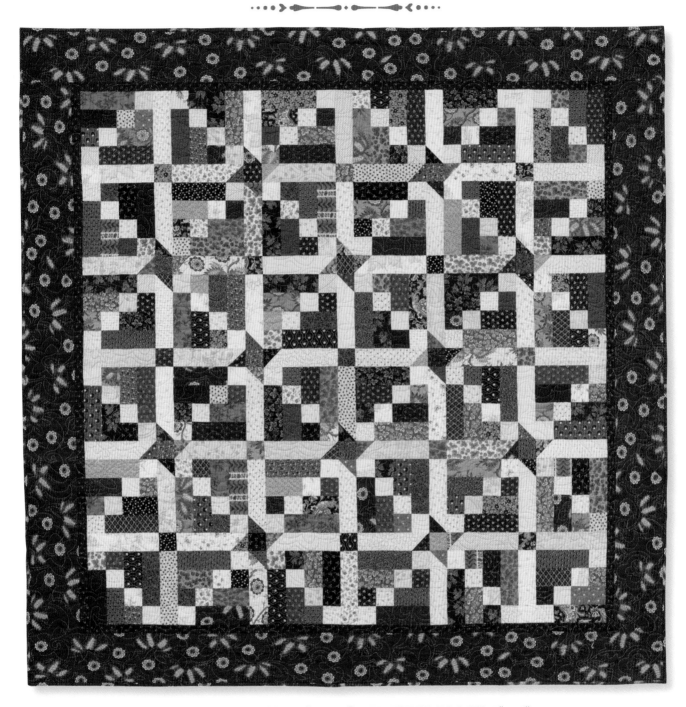

**FINISHED QUILT:** 71½" × 71½" • **FINISHED BLOCK:** 8" × 8"

*Designed by Kim Brackett; made by Mary Flynn*

*As welcoming as a tree-shaded hideaway beside a sun-dappled shore, this quilt glows with warm, rich reproduction prints. For a contemporary alternative, try using bright fabrics and cutting all of the cream squares and rectangles from a single light print.*

## Materials

*Yardage is based on 42"-wide fabric.*

31 strips, 2½" × 42", of assorted dark prints for blocks

24 strips, 2½" × 42", of assorted cream prints for blocks

⅓ yard of dark brown print for inner border

2 yards of red floral for outer border and binding

5 yards of fabric for backing

75½" × 75½" piece of batting

## Cutting

*All measurements include ¼"-wide seam allowances.*

**From *each* of 10 assorted dark print strips, cut:**
3 rectangles, 2½" × 6½" (30 total)
2 rectangles, 2½" × 4½" (20 total)
4 squares, 2½" × 2½" (40 total)

**From *each* of 10 assorted dark print strips, cut:**
2 rectangles, 2½" × 6½" (20 total)
3 rectangles, 2½" × 4½" (30 total)
4 squares, 2½" × 2½" (40 total)

**From *each* of 11 assorted dark print strips, cut:**
2 rectangles, 2½" × 6½" (22 total)
2 rectangles, 2½" × 4½" (22 total)
6 squares, 2½" × 2½" (66 total; 1 is extra)

**From *each* of 14 assorted cream print strips, cut:**
3 rectangles, 2½" × 8½" (42 total)
5 squares, 2½" × 2½" (70 total)

**From *each* of 10 assorted cream print strips, cut:**
2 rectangles, 2½" × 8½" (20 total; 2 are extra)
8 squares, 2½" × 2½" (80 total; 6 are extra)

**From the dark brown print, cut:**
6 strips, 1½" × 42"

**From the red floral, cut:**
7 strips, 6" × 42"
8 strips, 2½" × 42"

---

### CUTTING FROM SCRAPS

If you prefer to use scraps, follow the instructions below. See "Cutting" at left for instructions on cutting the borders and binding.

**From assorted dark prints, cut:**
72 rectangles, 2½" × 6½"
72 rectangles, 2½" × 4½"
145 squares, 2½" × 2½"

**From assorted cream prints, cut:**
60 rectangles, 2½" × 8½"
144 squares, 2½" × 2½"

---

## Making the Blocks and Sashing Units

Press the seam allowances as indicated by the arrows, or as otherwise instructed.

1 Sew a cream 2½" square to a dark 2½" × 6½" rectangle as shown. Make 72.

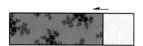

Make 72.

2 Sew together a dark 2½" square, a cream 2½" square, and a dark 2½" × 4½" rectangle as shown. Make 72.

Make 72.

3 Sew together two units from step 1 and two units from step 2 as shown. Make 36 blocks.

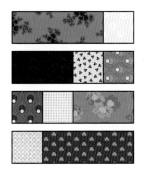 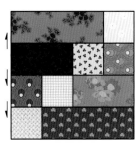

Make 36.

4 Draw a diagonal line from corner to corner on the wrong side of a dark 2½" square. Place the marked square on one end of a cream 2½" × 8½" rectangle, right sides together and corners aligned. Sew on the drawn line. Trim the excess fabric, leaving ¼" seam allowances, and press. Make 48.

Make 48.

## Assembling the Quilt Top

1 Arrange the blocks, the pieced sashing strips, the remaining cream 2½" × 8½" rectangles, and the remaining dark 2½" squares in rows as shown.

2 Sew the pieces together into rows; press. Sew the rows together and press the seam allowances in one direction.

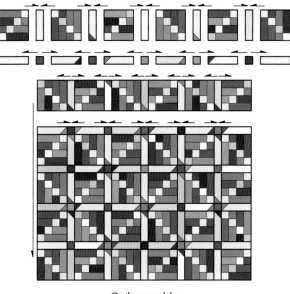

Quilt assembly

3 Sew the dark brown 1½"-wide strips together end to end. Measure the length of the quilt top through the center and cut two strips to this measurement. Sew the strips to the sides of the quilt top and press the seam allowances toward the borders. Measure the width of the quilt top through the center, including the borders just added, and cut two strips to this measurement. Sew the strips to the top and bottom of the quilt top and press the seam allowances toward the borders.

4 Repeat to add the red floral 6"-wide strips for the outer border.

## Finishing the Quilt

Refer to "Finishing Techniques" on page 236 for details on the following steps.

1 Layer and baste your quilt, and quilt as desired.

2 Using the red floral 2½"-wide strips, prepare and attach the binding.

# Hexagon Flowers Doll Quilt

**FINISHED QUILT:** 16" × 19½" • **FINISHED BLOCK:** 3½" × 3½"

*Designed and made by Kathleen Tracy*

*This little treasure was inspired by antique hexagon quilts from the 1800s, similar to Grandmother's Flower Garden quilts from the 1930s. The shapes for English paper piecing take a little time to prepare but are easily portable, making this a great take-along project.*

## Materials

*Yardage is based on 42"-wide fabric.*

12 scraps, at least 2" × 12" each, of assorted prints for outer hexagons

12 scraps, at least 2" × 2" each, of assorted prints for center hexagons

¼ yard of brown print for block backgrounds

¼ yard of green print for borders

⅛ yard of medium blue print for border corner squares

¼ yard of gold print for binding

⅝ yard of fabric for backing

20" × 24" piece of batting

Several sheets of cardstock or heavyweight paper

Single-hole paper punch (optional)

## Cutting

*All measurements include ¼"-wide seam allowances.*

**From *each* of the 12 assorted scraps for outer hexagons, cut:**

6 squares, 2" × 2" (72 total)

**From *each* of the 12 assorted scraps for center hexagons, cut:**

1 square, 2" × 2" (12 total)

**From the brown print, cut:**

12 squares, 4" × 4"

**From the green print, cut:**

2 strips, 3" × 11"
2 strips, 3" × 14½"

**From the medium blue print, cut:**

4 squares, 3" × 3"

**From the gold print, cut:**

2 strips, 1¼" × 42"

## Preparing the Hexagon Templates

You will need seven hexagon templates for each flower. Kathleen Tracy suggests making at least 28 and then using each one three times. To make the hexagon templates, you have several options.

**Make your own.** Use the pattern on page 225 to make a template. Then trace the template onto cardstock or heavy paper and cut out the hexagons carefully.

**Print hexagons from the Internet.** Kathleen has had success with a website (incompetech.com/graphpaper/hexagonal/) that allows users to print hexagons of any size. Print a grid of hexagons with sides equal to .6"; that's the size used to create the 3" flowers. Print directly onto cardstock and cut the hexagons apart individually.

**Purchase precut paper hexagons.** Several companies make paper hexagon shapes that you can purchase in different sizes to use as templates. You can find them at quilt shops, online, or at quilt shows. Choose hexagon templates that measure ⅝" along the sides, or 1" from flat side to flat side.

After the shapes are cut out, Kathleen recommends placing a dot in the center of each paper hexagon and using a single-hole punch to make a hole. The hole makes it easy to pin the templates to the fabric. It also makes it easy to remove the paper templates with the edge of a seam ripper after the pieces have been stitched together.

# Making the Blocks

For each hexagon flower, choose six matching squares for the petals and one contrasting square for the center.

1 Center a paper hexagon on the wrong side of a 2" square. Secure the paper to the fabric by placing a small pin through the hole. Cut around the shape, leaving a generous ¼" all around.

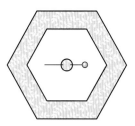

2 Fold one edge over and baste the corner as you fold over the next edge. Go around the hexagon, stitching down all the sides and being careful not to catch the paper. Finish with a knot to secure. Repeat for the six matching hexagons and the contrasting center hexagon. Leave the paper pieces inside.

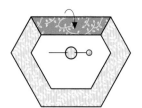 

Make 6 matching and 1 contrasting hexagon for each flower.

3 Place the center hexagon right sides together with another hexagon. Whipstitch the sides together, catching just the edges of the fabric.

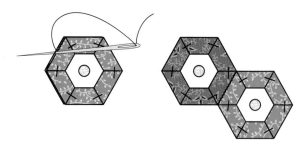

4 Continue adding the remaining hexagons around the edges of the center hexagon in a circular fashion.

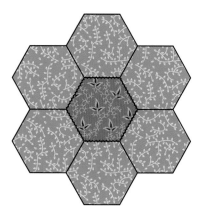

5 Connect the sides of the outer hexagons by placing them right sides together, folding the paper if necessary. When you've finished a flower, remove the paper hexagons and press flat. Repeat to make 12 hexagon flowers, reusing the paper templates as desired.

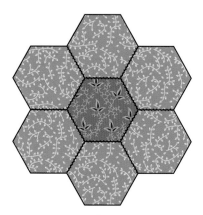

Make 12.

6 Center and appliqué a hexagon flower to each brown 4" square. Make 12.

Make 12.

## Assembling the Quilt Top

1 Lay out the blocks in four rows of three blocks each as shown.

2 Sew the blocks together into rows, pressing the seam allowances in opposite directions from row to row. Sew the rows together and press the seam allowances in one direction.

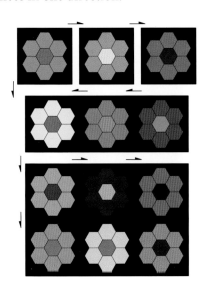

Quilt assembly

3 Sew the green 3" × 14½" strips to the sides of the quilt top. Press the seam allowances toward the borders. Sew a medium blue 3" square to each end of both green 3" × 11" strips and press the seam allowances toward the strips. Sew these to the top and bottom of the quilt top and press the seam allowances toward the borders.

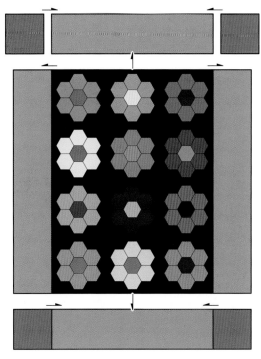

Adding borders

## Finishing the Quilt

Refer to "Finishing Techniques" on page 236 for details on the following steps.

1 Layer and baste your quilt, and quilt as desired.

2 Using the gold 1¼"-wide strips and referring to "Single-Fold Binding" on page 239, prepare and attach the binding.

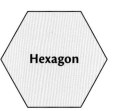

Hexagon

# Gettysburg Sun

**FINISHED QUILT:** 30" × 36¾" • **FINISHED BLOCK:** 5½" × 5½"

*Designed and pieced by Carol Hopkins; quilted by Lisa Ramsey*

*The three-day-long Battle of Gettysburg was fought under the hot July sun in 1863. The warm radiance of this quilt suggests happier days, and if you feel playful, keep in mind that the sun's center and points don't always have to match.*

## Materials

*Yardage is based on 42"-wide fabric.*

9 scraps, at least 8" × 10" each, of assorted gold prints for blocks (3 for suns, 6 for backgrounds)

11 scraps, at least 8" × 10" each, of assorted dark blue prints for blocks (5 for suns, 6 for backgrounds)

4 scraps, at least 8" × 10" each, of assorted gray prints for blocks (suns)

⅝ yard of dark blue print for inner border, cornerstones, and binding

⅛ yard of gold print for cornerstones

½ yard of green floral for sashing

½ yard of blue-and-gold large-scale print for outer border

1⅛ yards of fabric for backing

36" × 43" piece of batting

### SUNNY OPTION
Instead of using the same fabric for the sun's center and points, select a different fabric for the center of some blocks. The centers are a good place to showcase striped fabrics.

## Cutting

*All measurements include ¼"-wide seam allowances. Half of the blocks have gold or gray suns on dark blue backgrounds (block A), and half of the blocks have dark blue or gray suns on gold backgrounds (block B). Keep the fabrics for each block separate.*

### BLOCK A
*Cutting is for 1 block. You'll need 6 total (indicated by totals in parentheses).*

**From 1 gold or gray scrap for sun, cut:**
1 square, 3½" × 3½" (6 total)
2 squares, 2½" × 2½"; cut the squares in half diagonally to yield 4 triangles (24 total)
8 squares, 1⅜" × 1⅜" (48 total)

**From 1 dark blue scrap for background, cut:**
2 squares, 2½" × 2½"; cut the squares in half diagonally to yield 4 triangles (24 total)
4 squares, 1¾" × 1¾" (24 total)
8 rectangles, 1⅜" × 1¾" (48 total)
4 squares, 1⅜" × 1⅜" (24 total)

### BLOCK B
*Cutting is for 1 block. You'll need 6 total (indicated by totals in parentheses).*

**From 1 dark blue or gray scrap for sun, cut:**
1 square, 3½" × 3½" (6 total)
2 squares, 2½" × 2½"; cut the squares in half diagonally to yield 4 triangles (24 total)
8 squares, 1⅜" × 1⅜" (48 total)

**From 1 gold scrap for background, cut:**
2 squares, 2½" × 2½"; cut the squares in half diagonally to yield 4 triangles (24 total)
4 squares, 1¾" × 1¾" (24 total)
4 squares, 1⅜" × 1⅜" (24 total)
8 rectangles, 1⅜" × 1¾" (48 total)

*(Continued on page 228)*

*(Continued from page 227)*

## SASHING, CORNERSTONES, BORDERS, AND BINDING

**From the dark blue print, cut:**
10 squares, 2½" × 2½"; cut the squares in half diagonally to yield 20 triangles
4 strips, 1¾" × 42"
4 strips, 2" × 42"

**From the gold print, cut:**
10 squares, 2½" × 2½"; cut the squares in half diagonally to yield 20 triangles

**From the green floral, cut:**
31 rectangles, 1¾" × 6"

**From the blue-and-gold large-scale print, cut:**
4 strips, 3½" × 42"

# Making the Blocks

Both blocks are constructed in the same way. Make six *each* of blocks A and B. Press the seam allowances as indicated by the arrows, or as otherwise instructed.

1 Sew a triangle of sun fabric to a background triangle to make a half-square-triangle unit. Make four.

Make 4.

2 Cut each unit in half diagonally to yield eight triangles. Sew two pieces together to make an hourglass unit measuring 1¾" square, including seam allowances. Press the seam allowances open and trim the dog-ear corners. Make four.

Make 4.

3 Place a 1⅜" square of sun fabric on the left end of a background rectangle, right sides together. Sew diagonally across the sun square. Fold the resulting triangle toward the outer corner and press in place. Make four. Make four reversed units, sewing the square of sun fabric to the right end of the background rectangle.

Make 4.

Make 4.

4 Arrange and sew together one of each type of unit as shown. Make four matching units.

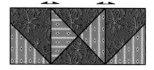

Make 4.

5 Place a 1⅜" background square on each corner of the 3½" square of sun fabric, right sides together. Sew diagonally across the background squares. Fold the resulting background triangles toward the outer corners and press.

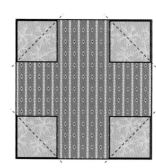 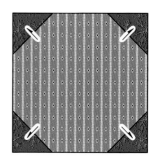

6 Arrange four 1¾" background squares with the side and center units as shown. Sew the pieces together into rows, and then join the rows. Make six each of blocks A and B measuring 6" square, including seam allowances.

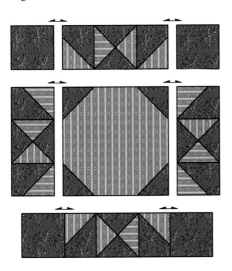

Block A
Make 6.

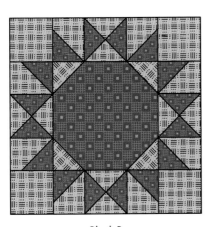

Block B
Make 6.

## Making the Cornerstones

1 Sew the dark blue and gold triangles together to make 20 half-square-triangle units.

Make 20.

2 Cut each unit from step 1 in half diagonally to yield 40 triangles. Sew two pieces together to form an hourglass unit. Press the seam allowances open and trim the dog-ear corners. Make 20 hourglass cornerstones measuring 1¾" square, including seam allowances.

Make 20.

## Assembling the Quilt Top

1 Lay out the blocks in four rows of three blocks each, arranging them with the sashing rectangles and cornerstones as shown.

2 Sew the pieces together into rows, and then join the rows.

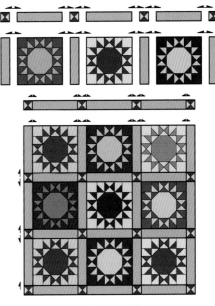

Quilt assembly

3 Measure the length of the quilt top through the center and trim two of the dark blue 1¾"-wide strips to this measurement. Sew the strips to the sides of the quilt top. Measure the width of the quilt top through the center, including the borders just added, and trim the remaining dark blue 1¾"-wide strips to this measurement. Sew the strips to the top and bottom of the quilt top to complete the inner border.

4 Measure the length of the quilt top through the center and trim two blue-and-gold 3½"-wide strips to this measurement. Sew the strips to the sides of the quilt top. Measure the width of the quilt top through the center, including the borders just added, and trim the remaining blue-and-gold 3½"-wide strips to this measurement. Sew the strips to the top and bottom of the quilt top to complete the outer border.

## Finishing the Quilt

Refer to "Finishing Techniques" on page 236 for details on the following steps.

1 Layer and baste your quilt, and quilt as desired.

2 Using the dark blue 2"-wide strips, prepare and attach the binding.

Adding borders

# Confederate Courtship

**FINISHED QUILT:** 84" × 105" • **FINISHED BLOCK:** 15" × 15"

*Designed and made by Evelyn Sloppy*

*Snowflake blocks and earthy hues prove to be perfect companions in this diagonally set beauty. Pull out lots of rust, green, brown, and tan reproduction fabrics from your stash, and round the corners for an elegantly simple finishing touch.*

## Materials

*Yardage is based on 42"-wide fabric.*
8 rust prints, ½ yard each, for blocks
8 green prints, ⅜ yard each, for blocks
8 brown prints, ⅜ yard each, for blocks
8 tan prints, ¾ yard each, for blocks
3 yards of tan floral for setting triangles
1 yard of fabric for binding
8 yards of fabric for backing
88" × 109" piece of batting

## Cutting

*All measurements include ¼"-wide seam allowances.*

**From *each* of the 8 rust prints, cut:**
1 strip, 3½" × 42"; crosscut into 8 squares, 3½" × 3½" (64 total)
2 strips, 2½" × 42"; crosscut into 24 squares, 2½" × 2½" (192 total)
2 strips, 1½" × 42"; crosscut into 40 squares, 1½" × 1½" (320 total)

**From *each* of the 8 green prints, cut:**
1 strip, 9½" × 42"; cut into:
- 1 square, 9½" × 9½" (8 total)
- 3 squares, 7½" × 7½" (24 total)
- 4 squares, 1½" × 1½" (32 total)

**From *each* of the 8 brown prints, cut:**
6 strips, 1½" × 42"; crosscut into:
- 6 strips, 1½" × 9½" (48 total)
- 6 strips, 1½" × 11½" (48 total)
- 6 strips, 1½" × 13½" (48 total)

**From *each* of the 8 tan prints, cut:**
1 strip, 9½" × 42"; cut into:
- 1 square, 9½" × 9½" (8 total)
- 3 squares, 7½" × 7½" (24 total)
9 strips, 1½" × 42"; crosscut into:
- 12 strips, 1½" × 4½" (96 total)
- 4 strips, 1½" × 6½" (32 total)
- 6 strips, 1½" × 9½" (48 total)
- 6 strips, 1½" × 11½" (48 total)
- 10 strips, 1½" × 13½" (80 total)

**From the tan floral, cut:**
4 strips, 24" × 42"; cut into:
- 4 squares, 24" × 24"; cut the squares into quarters diagonally to yield 16 triangles (2 are extra)
- 2 squares, 13½" × 13½"; cut the squares in half diagonally to yield 4 triangles

**From the binding fabric, cut:**
10 strips, 2½" × 42", or bias strips to total 388"

## Making the Snowflake Blocks

Press the seam allowances as indicated by the arrows, or as otherwise instructed.

1 From one rust print, gather eight 3½" squares and four 1½" squares. From one green print, gather one 9½" square and one 1½" square. And from one tan print, gather one 9½" square, four 1½" × 6½" strips, and four 1½" × 13½" strips.

2 On the wrong side of the tan 9½" square, mark two diagonal lines from corner to corner to make an X. Also mark vertical and horizontal lines through the center of the square. Layer the marked square on the green 9½" square, right sides together, and stitch ¼" from each side of both diagonal lines. Cut on all of the drawn lines to yield eight half-square-triangle units. Carefully press the seam allowances toward the green print.

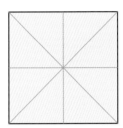 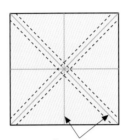

Cut on drawn lines.

3 On the wrong side of half of the units from step 2, draw a diagonal line from corner to corner. Layer one marked unit on one unmarked unit, right sides together and with contrasting fabrics facing each other. Butt the diagonal seams against each other and pin to secure. Stitch ¼" from both sides of the diagonal line, and then cut apart on the drawn line. Press the seam allowances to one side. Make eight quarter-square-triangle units and trim to 3½" square, including seam allowances.

4 Join two rust 3½" squares and two quarter-square-triangle units as shown. Make a total of four.

Make 4 for each block.

5 Join the four units from step 4 with four tan 1½" × 6½" strips and one green 1½" square as shown.

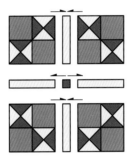 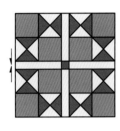

6 Join four tan 1½" × 13½" strips and four rust 1½" squares to the unit to complete one Snowflake block that measures 15½" square, including seam allowances. Repeat to make a total of eight Snowflake blocks, using one rust print, one green print, and one tan print for each block.

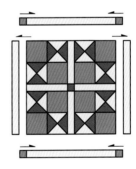 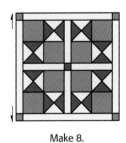

Make 8.

## Making the Surrounded Snowflake Blocks

**1** From one rust print, gather eight 2½" squares. From one green print, gather one 7½" square and one 1½" square. And from one tan print, gather one 7½" square and four 1½" × 4½" strips.

**2** Referring to steps 2 and 3 of "Making the Snowflake Blocks" beginning on page 232, use the tan 7½" square and the green 7½" square to make eight quarter-square-triangle units. Trim the units to 2½" square, including seam allowances.

**3** Referring to steps 4 and 5 of "Making the Snowflake Blocks," join the quarter-square-triangle units with the remaining pieces from step 1 to make a Snowflake block that measures 9½" square, including seam allowances. Make 24 Snowflake blocks.

**4** Using the three block diagrams at right as a guide, join three rounds of courthouse steps strips with cornerstones to each Snowflake block. Use assorted brown and tan strips that measure 9½", 11½", and 13½" in length and use rust 1½" squares for the cornerstones. Press the seam allowances of the strips toward the outside as you go. Make 16 Surrounded Snowflake blocks with two adjacent brown sides and two adjacent

tan sides. Make 4 Surrounded Snowflake blocks with three brown sides and one tan side. Make 4 Surrounded Snowflake blocks with three tan sides and one brown side. Each of the 24 blocks should measure 15½" square, including seam allowances.

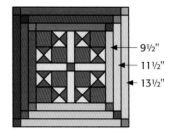

Make 16.

Make 4.

Make 4.

## Assembling the Quilt Top

**1** Arrange the Snowflake blocks, Surrounded Snowflake blocks, side setting triangles, and corner setting triangles into diagonal rows as shown at right.

2 Sew the pieces together into rows, and then join the rows. Add the corner triangles last, pressing the seam allowances toward the corners.

3 Trim the edges of the quilt top, aligning the ½" mark on the ruler with the block points.

## Finishing the Quilt

Refer to "Finishing Techniques" on page 236 for details on the following steps.

1 Layer and baste your quilt, and quilt as desired.

2 To make the quilt with rounded corners as shown in the photo on page 231, simply trim the corners using a dinner plate as a guide. Then use 2½"-wide bias strips to prepare and attach the binding. If you would like to leave the corners of the quilt square, you may use 2½"-wide straight-grain strips to bind the quilt.

Quilt assembly

# Finishing Techniques

Add borders to finish your quilt top. Add quilting and binding to your quilt, add a hanging sleeve if one is needed, label your quilt, and you're finished!

## Adding Borders

For best results, do not cut border strips and sew them directly to the quilt without measuring first. The edges of a quilt often measure slightly longer than the distance through the quilt center, due to stretching during construction. So measure the quilt top through the center, both lengthwise and crosswise, to determine how long to cut the border strips. This step ensures that the finished quilt will be as straight and as square as possible, without any wavy edges.

Many of the quilts in this book call for plain border strips. These strips generally are cut along the crosswise grain and seamed where extra length is needed. However, some projects call for the borders to be cut on the lengthwise grain so that they don't need to be pieced.

### BORDERS WITH BUTTED CORNERS

1 Measure the length of the quilt top through the center. From the crosswise grain, cut border strips to that measurement, piecing as necessary. Determine the midpoints of the border and quilt top by folding in half and creasing or pinning the centers. Then pin the border strips to opposite sides of the quilt top, matching the center marks and ends and easing as necessary. Sew the border strips in place. Press the seam allowances toward the border strips.

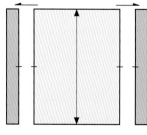

Measure center of
quilt, top to bottom.
Mark centers.

2 Measure the width of the quilt top through the center, including the side border strips just added. From the crosswise grain, cut border strips to that measurement, piecing as necessary. Mark the centers of the quilt edges and the border strips. Pin the border strips to the top and bottom edges of the quilt top, matching the center marks and ends and easing as necessary. Sew the border strips in place. Press.

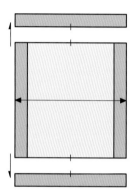

Measure center of quilt, side to
side, including border strips.
Mark centers.

### BORDERS WITH CORNER SQUARES

1 Measure the width and length of the quilt top through the center.

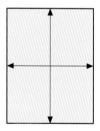

Measure center of quilt top
in both directions.

2 From the crosswise grain, cut border strips to those measurements, piecing as necessary. Mark the centers of the quilt edges and the border strips. Pin the side border strips to opposite sides of the quilt top, matching centers and ends and easing as necessary. Sew the side border strips to the quilt top; press the seam allowances toward the border strips.

3 Cut corner squares of the required size, which is the cut width of the border strips. Sew a corner square to each end of the remaining two border strips; press the seam allowances toward the border strips. Pin the border strips to the top and bottom edges of the quilt top. Match the centers, the seams between the border strips and corner squares, and the ends. Ease as necessary and stitch. Press.

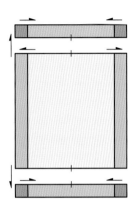

## Preparing to Quilt

If you'll be quilting your project by hand or on your home sewing machine, you'll want to follow these instructions for marking, layering, basting, and quilting. However, if you plan to have a professional machine quilter quilt your project, check with that person before preparing your finished quilt top in any way. Quilts do not need to be layered and basted for long-arm machine quilting, nor do they usually need to be marked.

### MARKING THE DESIGN

Whether you mark quilting designs on the quilt top or not depends upon the type of quilting you will be doing. Marking is not necessary if you plan to quilt in the ditch (along the seamlines) or outline quilt a uniform distance from seamlines. For more complex quilting designs, however, mark the quilt top before the quilt is layered with batting and backing.

Choose a marking tool that will be visible on your fabric and test it on fabric scraps to be sure the marks can be removed easily.

### LAYERING AND BASTING THE QUILT

Once you complete the quilt top and mark it for quilting, assemble the quilt "sandwich," which

consists of the backing, batting, and quilt top. The quilt backing and batting should be at least 4" to 6" longer and wider than the quilt top. For large quilts, it is usually necessary to sew two or three lengths of fabric together to make a backing that is large enough. Trim away the selvages before piecing the lengths together. Press the seam allowances open to make quilting easier.

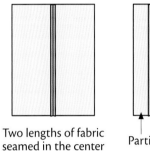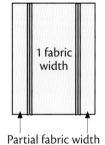

Two lengths of fabric seamed in the center          Partial fabric width

1 Spread the backing wrong side up on a flat, clean surface. Anchor it with pins or masking tape. Be careful not to stretch the backing out of shape.

2 Spread the batting over the backing, smoothing out any wrinkles.

3 Center the pressed quilt top on top of the batting. Smooth out any wrinkles and make sure the quilt-top edges are parallel to the edges of the backing.

4 Starting in the center, baste with needle and thread and work diagonally to each corner. Then baste a grid of horizontal and vertical lines 6" to 8" apart. Finish by basting around the edges.

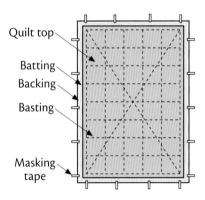

Quilt top
Batting
Backing
Basting
Masking tape

For machine quilting, you can baste the layers with #2 rustproof safety pins. Place pins about 6" to 8" apart, away from the areas you intend to quilt.

## Quilting

Some of the projects in this book were hand quilted, others were machine quilted, and some were quilted on long-arm quilting machines. The choice is yours! For more information on hand or machine quilting, refer to ShopMartingale.com/HowtoQuilt.

## Double-Fold Binding

Many of the quilts in this book use a French double-fold binding. Cut strips across the width of the fabric. Binding strips cut 2½" wide will result in a finished binding that's slightly more than ¼" wide. You will need enough strips to go around the perimeter of the quilt, plus 10" for seams and to turn the corners.

1 Sew the binding strips together to make one long strip. Join strips at right angles, right sides together, and stitch across the corner as shown. Trim the excess fabric and press the seam allowances open to make one long piece of binding.

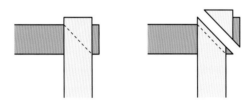

2 Fold the strip in half lengthwise, wrong sides together, and press.

3 If you plan to add a hanging sleeve, do so now before attaching the binding; see "Adding a Hanging Sleeve" on page 240.

4 Starting on one side of the quilt and using a ¼"-wide seam allowance, stitch the binding to the quilt, keeping the raw edges even with the quilt-top edge and leaving a 6" tail unstitched at the start. End the stitching ¼" from the corner of the quilt and backstitch. Clip the threads.

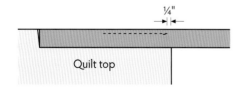

¼"

Quilt top

5 Turn the quilt so that you will be stitching down the next side. Fold the binding straight up, away from the quilt, making a 45° angle. Fold the binding back down onto itself, even with the edge of the quilt top. Begin stitching ¼" from the corner, backstitching to secure the stitches. Stitch to the next corner, stopping ¼" from the edge, and repeat the folding and stitching process. Repeat on the remaining edges and corners of the quilt.

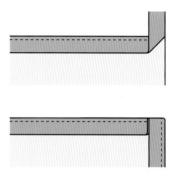

6 On the last side of the quilt, stop stitching approximately 7" from where you began. Remove the quilt from the machine. Overlap the ending binding tail with the starting tail. Trim the binding ends with a perpendicular cut so that the overlap is exactly the same distance as the cut width of your binding strips. (If your binding strips are 2½" wide, the overlap should be 2½"; for 2"-wide binding, the overlap should be 2".)

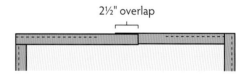

2½" overlap

7 Open up the two ends of the folded binding. Place the tails right sides together so that they join to form a right angle, as shown. Mark a diagonal stitching line from corner to corner and pin the binding tails together.

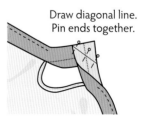

Draw diagonal line.
Pin ends together.

8 Stitch the binding tails together on the marked line. Trim the seam allowance to ¼"; finger-press the seam open to reduce the bulk. Refold the binding, align the edges with the raw edges of the quilt top, and finish sewing it in place.

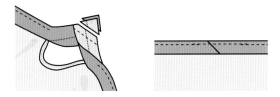

9 Fold the binding over the raw edges to the back of the quilt, with the folded edge covering the row of machine stitching. Hand stitch in place, mitering the corners.

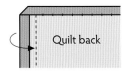 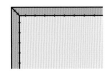

## Single-Fold Binding

Single-fold binding is a popular choice for small quilts, as some people feel double-fold binding is too heavy for small quilts and can contribute to a wavy edge. Some quiltmakers are thoroughly devoted to single-fold binding and use it for quilts of all sizes. To prevent the binding from stretching, use a walking foot or engage the dual-feed mechanism, if you have one built into your machine.

1 Cut the number and width of binding strips specified in the project instructions. The strip quantity needs to be enough to go around your quilt, plus 2" extra for seaming. Cut the strips crosswise (across the width of the fabric, from selvage to selvage). Using a diagonal seam, join the short ends, right sides together, to make one long piece. Press the seam allowances open.

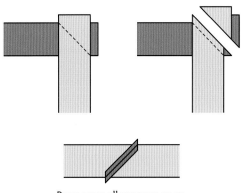

Press seam allowances open.

2 With right sides together, align a raw edge of the binding with the raw edge of the quilt. Beginning about 4" to 5" from the binding end, sew the binding to the quilt using a ¼" seam allowance. Stop sewing ¼" from the corner; backstitch and remove the quilt from the machine.

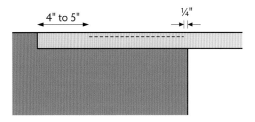

3 Rotate the quilt a quarter turn so you'll be ready to stitch the next side. Fold the binding up at a 90° angle.

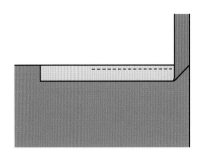

4 Next, fold the binding back down over the first fold and align the binding raw edge with the quilt raw edge. Reposition the quilt under the presser foot. Beginning with a backstitch, continue sewing the binding to the quilt top. Sew until you

are ¼" from the next corner; backstitch. Repeat the folding and stitching steps at each corner.

5 Stop sewing about 5" or 6" from the start. Remove the quilt from the machine.

6 Fold the beginning of the binding strip toward the center of the quilt at a 90° angle. Repeat, folding the end of the binding strip toward the edge of the quilt at a 90° angle, leaving about a ⅛" gap between the folds. Press. By leaving the gap, the binding will lie nice and flat.

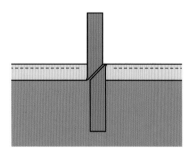

7 Align the fold lines, right sides together, and pin them in place. Sew on the fold line, backstitching at the beginning and end. Trim the excess binding strip, leaving a ¼" seam allowance. Press the seam allowances open. Finish sewing the binding in place.

8 Trim the batting and backing even with the quilt edges. Fold the binding away from the quilt and turn the raw edge under ¼". Fold the binding over the quilt edge and pin it in place so it covers the first stitches, mitering corners as you go when turning.

9 Blindstitch the binding to the quilt back, using small, closely spaced stitches and being careful not to stitch through to the front of the quilt. You may find it helpful to take three or four extra stitches on the folds of the mitered corners to hold them in place.

## Adding a Hanging Sleeve

If you plan to display your finished quilt on the wall, be sure to add a hanging sleeve.

1 Using leftover fabric from the quilt backing, cut a strip 6" to 8" wide and 1" shorter than the width of your quilt. Fold the ends under ½", and then ½" again to make a hem. Stitch in place.

2 Fold the fabric strip in half lengthwise, wrong sides together, and baste the raw edges to the top of the quilt back. The top edge of the sleeve will be secured when the binding is sewn on the quilt.

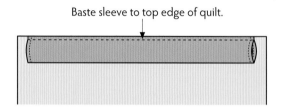
Baste sleeve to top edge of quilt.

3 Finish the sleeve after the binding has been attached by blindstitching the bottom of the sleeve in place. Push the bottom edge of the sleeve up just a bit to provide a little give; this will keep the hanging rod from putting strain on the quilt.

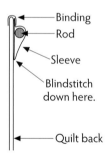

## Signing Your Quilt

Don't forget to sign and date your quilt. Future generations will be interested to know more than just who made it and when. Labels can be as elaborate or as simple as you desire. The information can be handwritten, typed, or embroidered. Be sure to include the name of the quilt, your name, your city and state, the date, the name of the recipient if the quilt is a gift, and any other interesting or important information about the quilt.